the rainbow
connection

the rainbow connection

cristina carlino

doubleday

new york   london   toronto   sydney   auckland

PUBLISHED BY DOUBLEDAY
a division of Random House, Inc.
1540 Broadway, New York, New York 10036

DOUBLEDAY and the portrayal of an anchor with a dolphin are trademarks of
Doubleday, a division of Random House, Inc.

Library of Congress Cataloging-in-Publication Data
Carlino, Cristina.
The rainbow connection / Cristina Carlino. — 1st ed.
p.   cm.
Includes bibliographical references.
1. Color—Psychic aspects.   2. Chakras.   3. Color—Therapeutic use.   I. Title.
BF1045.C6C37   1999   98-42349
131—dc21   CIP

ISBN 0-385-49387-8

To my parents,

Patricia and Mario,

thank you for giving me

the house of color, and thank you for giving me God.

May we be with each other for all eternity.

acknowledgments

To my mother, Patricia, and my father, Mario. I thank God for being given the nicest, sweetest, most extraordinarily kind parents, who always made me feel special. I realize now that they often gave to me what they had never been given themselves. To Michele, who lives in the house of blue rooms, I thank God for giving me a sister with an uncanny gift of gab. To my brother, "Saint" Mark, you will always be my hero. To my brother-in-law and business partner, David, I thank you for the past six years of sharing and building a legacy.

To my extended family, who stay in my heart. To my grandmother, Leona: you have never forgotten my birthday or holidays, even though I have forgotten yours. To my uncles and aunts and their beloved children; and a special thank you to my Uncle Dominic, for your infinite wisdom, and my godparents, Dorothy and George, for your courageous journey.

To my extended family at philosophy and BioMedic, you've shown me every day what it is that I love about people. Thank you for building the dream.

To our BioMedic doctors, nurses, and patients, thank you for your dedication in service and support of our company.

To our philosophy representatives, counter personnel, and customers, thank you for giving philosophy a presence in the land of the giants.

A very special thank-you to Elizabeth Harris and Carole Fisher for holding my world together in ways I cannot. I shall be eternally grateful to you both.

To Joyce Avalon, for seeing the rainbow and making it happen.

To Jack Friedland for going the distance.

To Bob Brink, who proves unequivocally the kindness of strangers. Thank you for providing me your guiding light.

To Kelly Chapman Meyer, what can I say, except that I love you, dear friend.

To Todd Headlee, your belief in me through the years has inspired me. You are a true blue friend.

To Steve and Melissa, you'll always be a part of me.

To Gwen Moon, for her love and healing energy.

To Anne and Rick Bresnahan for believing in BioMedic and making it happen.

To Caroline and Wayne Morong for believing in philosophy and making it happen.

To John Williams—you're the best hands in the business and the kindest employer I've ever had.

To Rich Ingle for your tireless work, patience, and creativity.

To the caretakers, Brett, Elizabeth, and David. I thank you for caring so deeply for those I love.

To the unsung heroes of this project. Christy Fletcher, for helping me feel safe in her hands. Janet Hill, for seeing the rainbow and making it happen. Andrew Stuart, for your patience, humor, and willingness to dance an abstract dance. Frances Jones, for getting into my soul and decorating my thoughts. A heartfelt thank-you to the dream team.

To O.W. Thanks so much for your kind words about philosophy®; your rainbow heart is a godsend.

To women in my past who gave me help when I needed it: Lois Miller, Connie Walters, Barbara Wyatt, Lillian Burns, Gwen Rains, Bonnie Zabel.

To Russell Chapman and Anna Lou Harmes. Thank you for your surrogate parenting.

To the guardian angels. Sarah, the creator. Emily, the lover. Matthew, the player. John, the genius. Jack, the leader, and little Kate, the beloved. Thank you for allowing me to see heaven through your eyes.

And finally, to Barry. Thank you is too small a phrase.

May God bless us all, and keep watch over us always.

Note: The fundamental concepts presented herein are part of an existing body of ancient wisdom. *The Rainbow Connection* is simply an offering of new interpretations and insights.

If you have been a subject of physical, sexual, emotional abuse, or are suffering from depression, you owe it to yourself to seek individual, professional advice, as this book cannot provide you the healing you require.

contents

part i

---

the rainbow connection

a colorful story

m y parents grew up in Gary, Indiana, a city that could easily be described as a place of "black and white" thinking, inhabited as it was by black and white people who lived apart from each other. My parents knew that there had to be a place in the world with less contrast and more color; for this reason, they realized that Gary could never be a permanent home. My parents, Patricia and Mario, were nineteen years old when they married, and by the time they were twenty they had their first child, my sister Michele. My mother worked at the steel mills during the early years of their marriage to support my father while he earned a degree in optometry. He would spend the rest of his years helping others to see better.

My father, mother, and sister decided to leave Gary after he received his degree, so they set their compass due west. With five hundred dollars to their names, they headed out of the past and into the future with hope, faith, and above all, love. Their journey eventually brought them to the Colorado state line, where the sign read WELCOME TO COLORFUL COLORADO. My dad, truly a man of vision, got out of the car and kissed the ground, knowing that he had found a home for his family, which at that point also included me, as I had already begun growing inside my mother. That colorful state was then and is now the most beautiful place I have ever known.

The family first settled in an area of Colorado Springs known as "The Garden of the Gods," where I was born six months later. We then moved from "The Garden of the Gods" to a place called "The Skyway District," where every street was named after something in the cosmos: Orion Drive, Jupiter Street, Constellation Boulevard. We lived on Hercules Drive, where I spent my formative years, the most magical years of my life.

Not only was the surrounding country colorful, but my new home truly was "The House of Color," and it was exceptional. My father and mother lived in the indigo and violet room: Their carpeting was a deep, rich shade of violet; the bedspread, along with the curtains, was a very soft shade of indigo; store-bought religious artifacts dominated the decor. My sister lived in the red room: The carpeting was bright cherry red; the walls and bedspread were pink; and the curtains were pink and covered with beautiful red roses.

My room was filled with shades of green and blue: The carpeting and the curtains were a crisp grass green; the walls were sky blue; and my bedspread was green with little blue love knots. Stuffed animals and a beautiful statue of the Virgin Mary draped in blue garments watched over my every move.

Our family bathroom was primarily white except for the blue bathtub, blue counters, and multicolored mosaic flooring. The living room was predominantly white with accents of gold and green, including a large green statue of Moses holding the Bible and a large gold lamp that featured Adam and Eve climbing up an apple tree. Adam and Eve were placed on an old stereo console that played the sound track to *The Sound of Music* almost every day. For this reason alone, the living room was my favorite room in the house. The kitchen's color scheme was a subdued mixture of browns, golds, and hints of yellow and orange. The only place I could find an abundance of yellow and orange was in my backyard, where the sun would shine. That backyard, which included a swing set, tricycle, and my pet duck Ozzie, represented my entire universe.

Our world was truly a colorful place. Come to think of it, the only thing black and white in that world was a black-and-white television set and the black-and-white newspaper delivered daily. Regardless of how the rest of the world saw their surroundings, we children, like God, saw things in full living color.

We had a charming, middle-class existence. Simple pleasures were our favorite pleasures. Before bedtime my father brought color into the darkness of the night by asking me to guess which object in our home he was thinking of; the only clue he gave me was the color of the object. His game helped put all my fears about the dark to rest.

My mother was so very, very sweet to me. She took care of my every need, and through her love and kindness taught me not to see people as good or bad, but to see that people deserved love no matter what. My mother also had extraordinary intuition: She insisted that I have a piano, despite the fact that no one in the family was musically inclined. This act of intuition provided a gift that has sustained me throughout my entire life, for wherever I go, my piano goes with me.

As for my sister, she couldn't stop talking. Even when we were separated within the house, she would insist that we continue communicating with one another through the air vents on the floors of our rooms (phones in children's rooms were unheard of in those days). My sister is still talking, and is absolutely the funniest and most beautiful woman I know.

However, the person I would come to revere most in my life was the person I prayed for the most when I was young. During my mother's third and final pregnancy, I prayed every night on my small knees that God would bring me a baby brother. God did better. God brought me a brother and delivered the family its saint. "Saint" Mark to be exact. The miracle of Mark completed the House of Color.

The best time in the House of Color was Christmas. Our Christmas came packaged with joy, laughter, presents, and, best of all, an aluminum Christmas tree with a special, plug-in, electric wheel. As the wheel turned, light was projected through spinning colors that made that Christmas tree dance in alternating shades of bright red, sunshine yellow, gorgeous green, and finally and forever, a deep shade of holiday blue.

Fast-forward to Christmas Day, 1994, a day that felt as if the best times in my life were now stuck in an old family photo album. My dancing aluminum Christmas tree and the House of Color were a million miles behind me. Alone, depressed, and fighting back sadness, I decided to climb a mountain near my house. My family had long disbanded, and each member had made new families, except for me. The people we had been were nothing like who we were now. My sadness was compounded by the fact that the person I most longed to be with that day chose to be somewhere else, with someone else. Needless to say, each step up that mountain became increasingly arduous as I carried the weight of the past with me. Eventually my tears became an obstacle to the climb, and I had to stop; there was no way I could conquer the mountain that day.

I found a small rock to sit on, closed my eyes, and tried to collect myself. Sun-showers delivered soft rain that helped to wash the tears down my face, while light from the sun was my only comfort. After a few minutes I opened my eyes, and in front of me was a beautiful, magnificent rainbow. Immediately, indeed miraculously, my feelings of sadness shifted to feelings of total reverence. God was revealed. The darkness became the light. The House of Color reappeared. I knew then as I know now—a clear, concise, direct message had been delivered to me. The message: gratitude. The interpretation: When we focus on the flaws or negativity in people, ourselves, or our experiences, the flaws and the negativity are exactly what we find. When we seek only the unique and positive color of a person, ourselves, or an experience, the rainbow reveals itself.

Although my family had left the House of Color, I could now see that each member had brought an important quality and lesson—their individual color—to my life, and that, collectively, they composed my rainbow. Today I know it is our family, friends, and mentors who guide us to our rainbow, and that the rainbow is unquestionably within us and outside of us; it is a metaphoric bridge that connects heaven and earth and us to each other, and the most important lesson we can learn is how to find the rainbow within ourselves. This concept is the basis of *the rainbow connection.*

When I descended the mountain that Christmas Day, I knew I had been given the ultimate gift: Whether or not I could see the path, God could see it for me. All mystical experiences can be judged by the fruit they bear. A new set of steps were to be taken, not on a mountain trail, but on a note pad. The fruit of my experience that day was the creation of philosophy, a personal-wellness company that emphasizes gratitude and the belief in miracles—and the ability to make them happen. As for the message of philosophy: We are never alone; not on holidays, not ever.

As you begin your journey, remember that when God is in your heart, God will be in your hands. Create with your hands, heal with your hands, touch with your hands, work with your hands, extend your hands, and pray with your hands. Know that there are no "coincidences," only acts of God, and that the rainbow is a miracle that lets us know unlimited potential does exist. May *the rainbow connection* help you discover your miracles, too.

introduction — the rainbow

God's plans for our lives are always so much better than our own. The day I stopped making plans, the plans began making me. By trusting in the mystery, my life became miraculous. Miracles occur when we align our soul, our heart, our thoughts, and our actions with conscious choice, and with God. We are beacons of light and, just like light, we are composed of a mix of seven colors not visible to the naked eye. These seven colors represent seven spiritual centers that must remain clear, balanced, and open to the unlimited vision of God and our unlimited potential to act as a spiritual channel for God's love and God's vision for us. How do you make a miracle happen? Let yourself out and let God in.

Recently a door was opened wide for me, and that was the publishing of this book. It would seem that the most likely book to come out of my professional experience—twenty years in the health and beauty industry—would surely be a beauty book. But I was never inspired to write such a book, because I knew better than anyone that real change comes from within and not without. Instead, I wanted to write a book that would guide people to believe in miracles: in themselves. Thus, when I was given the opportunity to write a book that might have demanded more formal and spiritual qualifications than I possessed, I felt obliged to do so, not because I thought I could but because I knew God would dot every *i*, cross every *t*, and give the project a voice that would flow through me and not from me.

While I do not possess professional credentials, by the grace of God I have been able to find my way around the world and establish a successful business that brings together my professional background and my personal interests. I have collected the spiritual tools that have enabled me to build the rainbow in my own life. My wish is to share this knowledge with others, to help them get on, and stay on, the road to spiritual empowerment. *the rainbow connection* is an exercise in the philosophy of life, color, and the miracle of positive energy. It answers the question of why, for some, the storm always bears a rainbow, and for others it continues on and on. *the rainbow connection* offers a colorized road map for those on the path to enlightenment and empowerment. It demands not your perfection but your constant attention to the flow of positive and negative energy and how it affects yourself and others. No longer will you dwell on the negativity of the past by blaming yourself and others. With the help of God and the seven colors of the rainbow, you will rebuild your individual House of Color by reinforcing the walls that are cracked, the doors that are broken, and by shedding light in the rooms that have remained dark. Doing so can create a spiritual transformation in your life that allows miracles to be a daily occurrence, not only in your life but in the lives of others.

why the rainbow?

The rainbow appears naturally in the presence of mist and light and brings together the seven primary colors of the spectrum in perfect harmony. This ephemeral entity is one of the most profoundly affecting and spectacular phenomena nature has bestowed upon us. Yet for those willing to open their eyes just a little wider, the rainbow offers a deeper message about unlimited potential. The rainbow is the only symbol in nature that connects heaven and earth and signifies the magic that is the promise of all creation. It is also a symbol of divine tolerance—the idea that we are all connected, regardless of race, ethnicity, or nationality. Each color of the rainbow represents a unique spiritual pathway, yet all pathways are honored as one since they lead to higher ground. There is no better demonstration of this connection than the fact that when all of the colors of the rainbow are combined equally, the result is pure light. Conversely, if the colors are combined in unequal proportions, the end result is muddy or dark.

As many of us remember from grade school, ROY G BIV was the key to memorizing the seven colors of the rainbow: red, orange, yellow, green, blue, indigo, violet. In *the rainbow connection* I will use the seven colors of the rainbow to discuss the seven primary spiritual centers I feel we all need to understand in order to achieve spiritual empowerment.

It is my belief that these seven spiritual centers correspond to the seven colors of the rainbow *and* that each of the colors has a core emotional issue attached to it. Consequently, an in-depth exploration of each color can bring you a greater understanding of these issues and their place in your own life. Following is an overview of the emotional issues and their correspondence to each other.

The earth tones (red, orange, yellow) of the rainbow provide our standard of life:

red = self-reliance

The affirmation is "I have." It explores what it is to have family, a code of ethics, balance, and security. It deals with having our material needs met.

orange = self-care

The affirmation is "I feel." It explores what it is to feel pleasure, joy, control, and a sense of well-being. It deals with having control over our emotional, physical, and sexual needs.

yellow = self-worth

The affirmation is "I can." It explores what it is to know self-worth, confidence, knowledge, and achievement. It deals with having our feelings of purpose and achievement fulfilled.

The connecting tone (green) bridges earth to heaven:

green = self-love

The affirmation is "I love." It explores the possibilities of peace, forgiveness, compassion, and generosity. It deals with our need to love and be loved. Green is considered the connecting tone because love is the solution to all problems.

The heavenly tones of the rainbow (blue, indigo, violet) provide our standard of virtue:

blue = self-expression

The affirmation is "I express." It explores the nature of sincerity, willpower, creativity, and communication. It deals specifically with our need to communicate and create honestly.

indigo = self-exploration

The affirmation is "I see." It explores the essence of intuition, imagination, choice, and inspiration. It deals with our ability to use our wisdom and intuition to see beyond our reality.

violet = selflessness

The affirmation is "I trust." It explores the nature of surrender, patience, faith, and gratitude. It deals with our need to surrender our will to a spiritual force that is larger than ourselves.

You may ask yourself what the benefit is of building your life around these seven colors and their corresponding qualities. Consider the following. If you were to combine all seven colors of the rainbow, not only would you get pure light, you'd probably get Oprah Winfrey. She positively embodies the seven colors of the rainbow in a profound way. She has used her position to spread knowledge, joy, tolerance, and love throughout the world and has made self-empowerment the guiding principle of her life's work. Like most colorful people, she has filled her life with many different kinds of people. She is undoubtedly one of our world's most powerful and enlightened leaders. By my standards, she has fulfilled the rainbow connection.

Bear in mind that being a superstar is not the goal of this program. Being a "super person" is. Oprah has skillfully demonstrated to the entertainment community and her fans that it is possible to be both.

On the surface, the rainbow connection would seem to lead from a "low" state to a "high" state: from physical and material concerns to spiritual and philosophical ones. Keep in mind, however, that the title of this book is *the rainbow connection,* not simply the rainbow. The goal of this book is to enable you to connect the colors together, to integrate all the stages into your life and to make sure they are all satisfied. It is not to focus on one to the exclusion of others. It would be a misinterpretation of this book to assume, for example, that because violet is at the apex of the rainbow, you don't need to worry about attending to your material or financial needs—a red issue. Each color of the rainbow represents a unique spiritual pathway, yet all pathways must be honored since they lead to your higher ground.

It is my hope that *the rainbow connection* will enable you to see yourself as a beacon of light by making you aware of the makeup of that light. The book provides a road map to help you build a fulfilling life through identifying your needs—you will learn how to build the rainbow in your own life. You will learn that building your red entails establishing fiscal responsibility and stable personal and familial bonds; that through building your orange you will take positive measures to take care of your emotional and physical well-being; that through building your yellow you will learn how to believe in yourself and achieve a strong sense of self-worth; that through building your green you will become a subscriber to the power of love and the profound effect it has in resolving all conflict; that through building your blue you will begin to express your truth creatively and verbally without fear of ridicule; that through building your indigo your specific information, knowledge, and inspiration can make the world a better place; and, finally, that through building your violet you will learn to live by the power of faith and not the power of people.

Without a plan we get lost. *the rainbow connection* will give you specific tools and guidelines to help build a better and more profound life and reveal the miracles in everyday existence.

In the chapters ahead, among other subjects, you will explore the following:

your roadblocks: dealing with denial
Discovering where you're stuck and moving on.

your journey: conscious choice
You will examine how your choices set your course.

your purpose: defining need vs. want

your road map: the seven colors of the rainbow

This section will briefly interpret the meaning of the seven colors of the rainbow. A quiz will help you reveal the current status of your emotional and spiritual outlook.

your fuel: how positive energy enables you, negative energy disables you

This section will teach you how to go with the flow, how to empower your life with positive affirmations, and how color can energize your spirit.

your traveling companion: your divine child

This section will reintroduce you to your "child consciousness." You will be taught how to bring the enchantment and magic back into your life by seeing life through the eyes of your "child."

your traveling essentials: incorporating mother nature

This section will teach you how to bring Mother Nature back into your daily life through the (common) senses. A special section will show you how to use the (uncommon) sense of intuition. You will be provided with twenty-eight affirmation/oracle cards that correspond to the specific emotional issues related to the seven colors of the rainbow. The cards will be used daily to direct you intuitively to spiritual and emotional issues with which you need to deal.

your daily prayers: daily meditations

This section will reinforce the power of positive affirmations.

your destination: house of color

This section will provide you with a fill-in chart that gives you an overview of those people, places, or things that positively make up your House of Color.

the colors: red, orange, yellow, green, blue, indigo, and violet
This section devotes one chapter per color for an in-depth view of where you are in relation to the energy of each color. Each chapter will tackle four specific issues related to your emotional and spiritual life. A journal section is provided in each chapter. Specific questions will be asked whose answers will enable you to identify those people, places, and things that are working for or against you.

maintenance: the road ahead
This section will help give you guidance in maintaining the rainbow connection in your life.

This book is your opportunity to evaluate where you are today in relation to the rainbow, and how you can reconnect with the power of God. It is for people who want to touch the sky because they've raised the bar to the appropriate rainbow-high level. It asks that you look at yourself and your life honestly so that your true, unlimited potential can be realized. It asks that you not judge yourself or others. It demands that you give to yourself whatever your parents were unable to give to you. And it instructs you to move toward the light and to forgive and release the darkness—a difficult act necessitating tremendous courage. But moving away from darkness will take you off the paths that lead nowhere and toward the path that leads you to the light, your spiritual destiny.

We live in an age that cries out for a renewal of belief, hope, and spirit. Our historic moment is marked by a daunting combination of promise and peril. We've come so far, in so many ways—technologically, economically, scientifically—yet we have somehow managed to lose sight of one of our greatest capacities as humans: the ability to believe in miracles and to make them happen.

My highest hope for this book is that it allows you the space to believe again, as you did when you were a child running toward the source of that luminous rainbow, hoping to catch it, feel it in your hands, and take it home with you. Starting today, you're through listening to people who tell you that you can't catch rainbows: I'm here to tell you that you can.

your journey: choosing consciously

philosophy: you can take the high road
or you can take the low road, it's your choice.

The promise of the rainbow is unlimited potential: you. You already have all you need to make miracles happen. The goal of *the rainbow connection* is to help you to connect to your potential, to give you the information you need to allow the song of your soul to be heard. When you begin to embody the strengths made manifest in the seven colors of the rainbow, your dreams, intentions, and desires become realities.

Before you begin, then, it is important to step back and look at your reality vs. your dreams. Personally, I often remind myself of the saying "Be careful what you wish for, because you just might get it." Certainly, in order to avoid a dubious fate we must be conscious of the desires behind the intentions we plan to set in motion. I've learned over the years that our intentions should always include God, because God chooses wisely for us and God empowers choices that include a higher purpose. And no matter what, God never, and I do mean never, lets us down. When we choose God over everything else, we choose the most powerful partner of all.

Choices that don't include God are disenfranchised from the get-go and, to my mind, are ticking time bombs that either explode or fizzle. Yet regardless of where your life is, do not despair, for God, with your help, can repair anything. If you are reading this book and find that you are either at a crossroads or in a paralyzing emotional state, do not hesitate to embrace it and, consequently, learn from it. Depression, discomfort, compulsive behavior, addiction, anger, sadness, lethargy, and suffocation are the ways your soul tries to get your attention. Your soul weeps: "This is wrong for me." "I deserve better." "I am on the wrong path." "I am unfulfilled." "I am fulfilling another's destiny, and not my own." "I need to change my life."

This book, God willing, will give you the courage to do the hardest thing in the world:

Admit your mistakes and weaknesses.
Take responsibility by making conscious choices.
Change your life by discovering your higher purpose.

All of which can be difficult as they often require you to move away from people, places, and activities that are the most familiar parts of your environment. However, nothing is impossible and no decision can be wrong if you:

Make God your partner.

philosophy: hope is desperation, faith is relaxation

Your days of wanting or hoping for miracles are over. You have begun a journey of faith, so relax.

P.S. If you are a person who believes in the power of science versus the power of God, this book can still be of great value to you. It is my belief that God and science coexist beautifully with one another. In this respect, I am reminded of sentiments expressed by the great physicist Stephen Hawking: "We can explain space, but we can't explain why it is there in the first place."

Perhaps God can.

your purpose: defining need vs. want

philosophy: if being rich makes you happy, why aren't the richest people the happiest?

Ideally, it shouldn't take a near-death experience or a tragedy to see the purpose of your life. In an ideal world, I believe the answer to "What do you believe the purpose of life is?" would be, "To live in love, in light, and to live life fully."

Unfortunately, too many of us detour from the path lit by the light of God. We become believers in fate, abandoning conscious choice and the wisdom inherent in our hearts and souls. We become unable to differentiate between "need" and "want," put our trust in our own intelligence, operate out of self-love, and cease to trust in God's intelligence and love.

One of the detours this often leads to is the ego-based path that has a singular destination point: me, myself, I. This journey is filled with I-centered decisions that make us take jobs that pay well versus jobs that are labors of love. We choose partners who fulfill our intellectual or economic needs and run away from those who might provide spiritual sustenance. We embark on a journey of total disempowerment—even if we are "masters of the universe"—because the motivation behind the journey is not to serve a greater good, it is only to serve ourselves. The only voice we hear is the one saying "What about me?"

Another blind alley is provided by the head trip. On this journey we are motivated solely by fear-based decisions; decisions that have been influenced by voices around us that cry, "You're nothing! You'll never make it! Why bother? You're a loser! You're lucky to have me." This path leads the ego-impaired person to believe in everyone but himself. He is on everyone's team but his own.

Too often these voices are so loud they drown out the voices of the heart and soul. It is my hope that your journey to the rainbow will help you to recognize the voices that are misleading you, help you tap into and balance your seven spiritual energy centers, and help you to clearly hear the voice of God that whispers, "You are divine. You are a miracle. Now go and make your miracles happen."

your expectations and your needs

"Need" and "want" are a funny thing. There is a major difference between the two. "Want" is the cry of the ego or head, and "need" is the song of the soul or heart. As an example, we may "want" to be rich, but what we really need is to be "free" of financial debt. That doesn't require being rich, it requires responsibility. To that end, take a moment to establish your real "needs" by filling out what you have, and what you "need."

family relations	want	need
parents	_____	_____
spouse	_____	_____
partner	_____	_____
children	_____	_____

material		
car	_____	_____
house	_____	_____
clothing	_____	_____
miscellaneous	_____	_____

financial	want	need
job	_____	_____
checking	_____	_____
savings	_____	_____
debt	_____	_____

physical

fit	_____	_____
healthy	_____	_____
sexually active	_____	_____
sports/recreation	_____	_____

social

friends	_____	_____
entertainment	_____	_____

travel

retreats	_____	_____
vacations	_____	_____

intellectual

professional degree	_____	_____
vocational degree	_____	_____
computer literate	_____	_____
reading	_____	_____
other	_____	_____

volunteer work

community	_____	_____
one on one	_____	_____
other	_____	_____

creative outlets	want	need
cooking		
gardening		
writing		
singing		
painting		
other		

spiritual
congregation		
affiliation		
meditation		

p r a y e r

The ability to differentiate between what you have and what you need begins to provide the light needed to see your rainbow. Your needs can be fulfilled when you take the responsibility of consciously choosing to ensure that they are met. There is no magic needed, just the willingness to look clearly at yourself and the determination to do what's best for your soul. The miracles begin when the song of your soul is awakened. Miracles are God's gifts to you. All you need is a heart and soul that are open to receive them.

your roadblocks: dealing with denial

philosophy: don't be afraid . . .

What change in your life are you most afraid of making?

Whatever you answered is your answer. This is what you need to do.

There is a classic moment in the movie *The Horse Whisperer* when the character Tom Booker says, "Knowing is the easy part, saying it out loud is the hard part." That one line is a real smack in the forehead, because many of us stay stuck in toxic or immobilizing situations although we know we really don't belong there. And why do we do this? FEAR.

Fear is negative. Fear is often unfounded. Fear causes us to react to situations versus responding to them. Fear creates immediate conflict, as we tend to project whatever is frightening us onto other people. We accuse, we berate, we retreat, we cave in, we stay stuck, and, more than anything, we lose our power. My friend, it's time to become a warrior. Take a stand. Rise out of the pile of garbage you've surrounded yourself with and take your first step. Yes, it smells. Yes, it's messy. No, it won't be easy, but you have only two choices. Stay and rot, or get a little messy and change your life. It's not going to be easy. Among other things, fear can be comfortable; often it's easier to stay with our old fears rather than take a chance and risk confronting new ones. Yet that is precisely what you, me, and the world need to do.

But before you can overcome the fears that have you stuck in the mud, you need to know what it is you are afraid of. If you feel stuck or immobilized but can't figure out why that is or how to begin to change, answering the following questions can provide insight. First, however, it's important to make the decision to be both openhearted and honest with yourself as you answer the questions. Confronting your fears and perceived limitations is difficult and sometimes painful, and answering some of these questions honestly may make you uncomfortable. But remember, confronting a fear enables you to move past it—and often it's the dread of the confrontation rather than the confrontation itself that is most paralyzing. As we all know from the times we have procrastinated, doing the job is never as bad as the dread we feel when we put off tackling it. Although these questions may be difficult to answer, they will help you understand your unconscious choices.

red / issue: self-reliance

Why are you afraid to be alone?

_____

_____

_____

_____

_____

Why do you sometimes alienate yourself from other people?

_____

_____

_____

_____

_____

Why are you occasionally greedy?

_____

_____

_____

_____

Why do you sometimes take from others without asking?

Why do you occasionally spend money you don't have?

Why is your life disorganized?

Why do you sometimes behave aggressively or passively?

Why do you occasionally feel you are better than others?

Why do you sometimes feel you are different from others?

Why are you occasionally prejudiced?

orange / issue: self-care

Why do you treat yourself badly?

Why are you sometimes sad?

Why are you sleeping your life away?

Why do you feel like not exercising or moving your body?

_____

_____

_____

Why are you abusing _____? (e.g., food, alcohol, drugs)

_____

_____

_____

_____

Why are you staying in an unhappy situation?

_____

_____

_____

_____

Why do you sometimes allow yourself to fall apart?

_____

_____

_____

_____

Why are you sometimes afraid of intimacy?

_____

_____

_____

_____

yellow / issue: self-confidence

Why do you occasionally allow others to treat you badly?

_____

_____

Why are you afraid of failing?

Why are you afraid of succeeding?

Why don't you believe in yourself?

Why are you sometimes afraid to lead?

green / issue: self-love

Why is it difficult to love yourself?

Why can't you make peace with those who have betrayed you?

_____

_____

_____

_____

Why do you treat certain people around you so poorly?

_____

_____

_____

Why are you occasionally envious or jealous?

_____

_____

_____

Why is it sometimes difficult to love others?

_____

_____

_____

_____

blue / issue: self-expression

Why do you have trouble keeping your commitments?

_____

_____

_____

Why do you sometimes tell little lies?

Why do you occasionally tell big lies?

Why are you unable to say what you really feel?

Why have you stopped being creative?

Why do you think your ideas aren't good?

Why do you take credit for other people's ideas?

_____

_____

_____

_____

indigo / issue: self-exploration

Why don't you act on your intuition?

_____

_____

_____

Why do you feel uninspired?

_____

_____

_____

Why are you afraid of learning new things?

_____

_____

_____

Why must you always be right?

_____

_____

_____

Why are you unable to make decisions?

_____

_____

_____
_____
_____

violet / issue: selflessness

Why do you obsess over every detail in your life?

_____
_____
_____
_____

Why do you sometimes try to control others?

_____
_____
_____
_____

Why is trust difficult for you?

_____
_____
_____
_____

Why don't you trust God?

_____
_____
_____
_____
_____

beyond fear: obsessing

If you feel that you know what your fears are, but you are still not making any changes, it may be because you are obsessing instead of trusting God. I call obsessing the "what if" syndrome, and often find that it is the ultimate formula for sabotage. The obsession of "what if this happens" or "what if that happens" has you so badly paralyzed that you are unable to make a decision or, for that matter, stay with a decision once it has been made.

Here's an example of what happens when the "what if" syndrome is applied to a romantic relationship:

What if I leave my lover and the next one is worse?

What if I stay and we get married?

What if my boyfriend doesn't ask me to marry him?

What if I get married and we get divorced?

What if he cheats on me?

What if I cheat on him?

What if I find someone I like better?

What if he is not the one?

The list could go on forever.

I believe that both obsession and fear stem from a lack of faith. How can we acquire faith? Faith is found in the color violet— its lessons help us to eliminate fear and obsession from our lives. It's important to read this book all the way through in order to confront the fears and issues raised by each color, and it is violet that allows us to release them once they are known.

overcommitted

Right now you may be thinking, "It's all well and good to say 'Confront your fears,' but at the moment I have a lot of other things to do!" I understand that. You work, you may have kids, and you may or may not have a partner. You feel as if you have too much to do and too little time to do it. Your relationship with your partner works sometimes and at other times not at all. Perhaps you don't have a relationship or, God forbid, you are in a bad one. Some days you may just want to run away, but where would you go, and who would be there to take care of everything?

Luckily, however, you thought enough of yourself to purchase this book. It's an important step toward taking care of yourself and believing in your desire and ability to move forward. This same self-care is something you need to incorporate into each day. Because when we nurture ourselves, we relax, and when we're relaxed it's easier to say, "I'd like to change" or "I need to grow." Consequently, I am going to give you very specific advice before you continue reading, because you need to take small steps to reinvest in yourself. These steps will provide daily reminders that you are valuable and worthy of being cherished, and that you *can* confront your fears, get out of the mud, and manifest each color of the rainbow.

• First suggestion: You cannot do this without God's help and guidance. If you do nothing else suggested in this book, do at least this: Ask God to help you each and every day.

• You can do nothing effectively without proper rest and a healthy diet. Although it is sometimes difficult to stick with balanced nutrition—quick fixes are seductive—it's important not to pursue anything in excess. Stop starving yourself with fad diets that don't work. Stop stuffing yourself with foods that are bad for you. Stop beating up on yourself about how you look. Genetics are out of your control. Eat well. Be good to yourself. If you're stressed out, don't compound it by stimulating yourself with caffeine or depressing yourself with alcohol.

• If you have children, wake up twenty to thirty minutes earlier. This is your chance for meditation and/or prayer time. Further advice on how to use this time effectively is on page 90.

• You don't have time for spas, but you probably do have time for a morning shower. Treat yourself to a body brush and a fragrant body wash. This two-minute treatment will make you feel pampered and invigorated. It's a wonderful way to start your day.

• Simplify your life by creating "uniforms" for yourself, clothes in which *you* are comfortable and which you know look well on *you*. Don't make yourself crazy trying to keep up with all the latest fashions.

• Simplify your life by simplifying your hair and makeup. Keep hand cream and nail file at your desk or bedside. Despite the color polish may add, skip it; you really don't have time.

• Create a more positive work environment. Ask permission to keep a plant and a small candle burning at your desk. Keep photos of the people you love nearby. If allowed, play your favorite music softly to reduce your stress level.

• Take work breaks. Get out of the office at least once or twice a day to take a few deep breaths of fresh air. Take a short, ten-minute walk, if possible.

• If you commute, inspirational books or tapes are a wonderful way to enhance travel time. Under no circumstances should you be listening to the news; you have enough to worry about.

• Evening routine: Collect yourself. Ask God to help you with the dinner, baths, homework, chores, and getting your children to bed. Do whatever you can to be extremely positive both verbally and physically with your kids and partner. Try and say a daily prayer, preferably before dinner is served, to remind your family how good your life is and how thankful you are. If it is impossible to sit down to dinner together, take a few moments before everyone goes to bed.

• Bedtime: It has been my experience that people want to take care of themselves, but they are just too wiped out before they fall asleep. I think it goes without saying that we all brush our teeth before going to bed. Do whatever you can to get into the habit of also treating yourself to a one-minute shower or a quick bath. After doing so, retreat to your bedroom. Agree to keep the television off. Play soft music, if necessary, to calm yourself down. Music from movie soundtracks can be magical. A few of my favorites include: *The Piano, Oscar and Lucinda, The Prince of Tides*. If you have a partner who is open to dancing, or even if you are alone, I believe dancing is the song of the soul. It's perfectly okay to dance to the music, turn to the music, and stretch out your arms like a ballerina. You will feel free and alive. You will pulsate with sensuality.

• Keep your facial moisturizer, eye cream, lip balm, and body lotion at your bedside. There is no reason you can't apply these products to clean skin in a reclining position.

It's important to remember that taking care of yourself is not selfish, it's the kindest thing you can do for those around you. It enhances you, enabling you to bring the best in yourself to the world and those around you.

immobilization

Sometimes it's hard not to feel trapped by our circumstances. We know we aren't happy with ourselves or our situation, but we can't begin to imagine a way to change. In these situations it's important to factor in two things: the value of small steps and a positive mind-set. Too often, when we think of change we think globally and—while it's important to keep the big picture in mind—it can often provide as much discouragement as encouragement. The top of the mountain is very far away when we are at the bottom. In these times the best thing you can do is to keep in mind that even one step a day will get you to the top eventually. And when you are tempted to stop climbing—to stop looking for the rainbow—turn to those who have persisted despite seemingly insurmountable obstacles: Helen Keller, FDR, Stephen Hawking, Christopher Reeve (whose book, *Still Me,* is a must-read). Learn from their examples and let their spirits buoy your steps on each phase of your journey.

the condemned

You are ashamed of your life, your past, and even your present. The choices you have made, in the eyes of others and even in your own eyes, are deplorable. In the worst-case scenario you are either in prison, on the run, or in a living hell. Now is not the time to write yourself off. Do not give up. Give in. Surrender to God. God does not judge. God loves you no matter what and asks that you do the same. Forgive yourself regardless of your past deeds. Each day just say one simple prayer: "Dear God, please lead me to higher ground." If you want, write this down and put it where you will see it daily.

the devastated

How does a parent bury a child? How does a young newlywed reconcile the untimely death of a spouse? How does a person come to terms with a devastating betrayal by another human being? The book *When Bad Things Happen to Good People* by Rabbi Harold S. Kushner says it better than I ever could. We must forgive. We must move forward. We must put our faith in God. We must seek help and not solitude, for I believe the solitude is the enemy. It gives us too much time to think. We must reach out and let others in. We must heal by doing the unthinkable, and that is helping another more desperate than ourselves. Love heals. Love saves. Love revives. We must be grateful for that which has been left behind, and we must have the faith to move on.

the self-righteous

You're never wrong. Your way is the highway, and the only way, as far as you're concerned. You've gone from believing in yourself to worshipping yourself. You see yourself as a big success, a beacon of light, or maybe an earth angel. But are you really?

Maybe success caused you to lose your humility. Is your beacon of light blinding to those who feel less special? As an earth angel, aren't there certain times you could admit you've been less than angelic in thought or deed? It's okay. As a spiritual being it's okay to be challenged by human experiences that cause us to be less than our spiritual best.

the unforgiving

We all must forgive. To not forgive is to stay stuck in negativity. Forgiving others releases negative energy from your life and opens your heart to love.

the codependent

They used to call it caring. Now the new word is codependency, and we all fit the profile to one degree or another. For those of you who "overcare" and believe that unless you provide, unless you stay, unless you pay the bills, unless you are there to hold everything together, things will just fall apart—get a grip. The only thing falling apart is you, for in your effort to solve every problem for others you have created enormous problems for yourself.

leave the guilty party

How can you drop their baggage? They will be so upset. How can they survive without you? You can't hurt them, but hey, it's no problem hurting yourself, right? I strongly believe that codependent people desperately need as much help as the people they are trying to help. Most codependents focus only on "the other person's life," "the other person's needs," "the other person's problems." Getting out of these situations is extremely difficult. But as far as I'm concerned, it's a life-or-slow-death situation for you. Ask yourself this, If someone were to tell you that you were sick and were going to die within a year, would others' "needs" still seem greater than your needs? Unlikely. You deserve your own life, to pursue your own dreams. You were not put on this earth to fulfill the dreams of others. You can listen to them, you can encourage them, but *they* need to pursue their goals. Weak-willed people are more than happy to let you carry their load. It's up to you to put down their baggage. And, ironically, this is often the kindest and most helpful thing you can do.

Try these thoughts on for size:

I am not guaranteed tomorrow.

I am here to fulfill a purpose.
God will lead me to that purpose if I listen.

And P.S. God, please help me to have the humility to realize I can't solve other people's problems.

conclusion

For the record, if you are batting a thousand and feel as if all these categories describe you, do not despair. The greatest fallacy in life is that we can't change, and yet that's all we do. We change age, diet, weight, partners, jobs, cities, friends, clothes, hair, and makeup. The list goes on. And believe it or not, you can change today and the way you feel about the future simply by changing your attitude from doom and gloom to songs and sunshine. It's the difference between being reactive and being proactive. The present is exactly that, a present. Are you ready to open it?

your road map: the seven colors of the rainbow

philosophy: without a plan, we get lost.

$g$od speaks to us through so many mediums, including mathematics, science, music, literature, nature, and yes, even color. *the rainbow connection* is an outgrowth of my many years spent surveying religion, philosophy, and quite frankly, people. The ideas in this book and the description of the seven colors are not the sketches for a new religion or the product of clinical research. Rather they are based on a strictly personal formula that has provided me with a way to seek personal enlightenment, empowerment, and a truly miraculous life.

On a figurative and literal level, *the rainbow connection* offers you a template for the emotional and spiritual empowerment we all seek. By using the rainbow, the only metaphor in nature that connects heaven and earth, you can see how we alone create our own heaven on earth—or hell on earth—through our feelings, our actions, our thoughts, and our beliefs. As you begin your journey to the rainbow, remember that the quality of that journey will be only as good as the intentions you put into each step you take.

So what is the first step? The first step is to be clear on what your soul needs. Yet when you ask most people to tell you what they need out of life, they are unable to answer specifically. Why? I believe most people are afraid to answer it honestly. And why is that? Because the honest answer is "I need everything," and often we feel guilty for thinking that. My personal belief, however, is that God puts no limits on our lives, so why should we? In order to change our lives from the ordinary to the extraordinary, we must first shift our thinking, and the most important mind change we must make is not "I can have it all," but "I deserve to have it all." If you believe you deserve it all, keep reading. If you don't believe "you deserve it all," put this book down right now; it is not for you.

For those of you who survived the last sentence and are still with me, your greater potential awaits you. Beginning now you must believe that you are no longer "a wannabe," but rather "a miracle" waiting to be revealed and you must realize that having it all, at least in this book, has nothing to do with the material world and everything to do with the spiritual world. The miracles you are meant to experience cannot be revealed, however, unless you make a commitment to make them happen. If you are someone who is living by fate, I genuinely believe you are postponing your life. You are *waiting* for things to happen instead of *making* things happen. And living by fate is to live by chance, and that is too Las Vegas for me and you. If you are someone who is willing to live by conscious choice, then your miracles are already in progress. Every choice you've ever made up until this paragraph is responsible for where you are. If you don't like where your life is today, make a choice to change it by using the metaphor of the rainbow to lead the way.

Why rainbows, you may ask? Why should seven colors have anything to do with me? If you believe that God has connected every dot in our universe, then you can believe that the rainbow is connected to us in a profound and mysterious way. God created our world so that no living matter could exist without light or water. And when you combine light and water, that combination produces many things over time, but it produces a rainbow instantly. In the same way, choosing to believe in your rainbow connection will allow you to begin making conscious choices and changes that will bring immediate benefits to your life. What proof do I have that this is true? Examples of some of the uses of the rainbow and its many profound implications have long been recognized by the Indians, both Native American and Hindu. For many years they have understood how each color of the rainbow connects to one of the seven primary energy centers that runs from the bottom to the top of our spine. According to ancient Indian teachings, these seven energy centers in the human body govern the generation and processing of energy in order to maintain our physical, emotional, and spiritual systems. They are responsible for who and what we are, how we look at things, what we like, and why we act the way we do. Recently a breakthrough bestseller, *Anatomy of the Spirit* by Caroline Myss, gave readers an in-depth medical perspective of this aspect of the body's unique energy system. I highly recommend it for anyone on the path to health and healing. The diagram at the back of the book better illustrates this concept. For further information on the Hindu system of energy, please refer to page 315 in the Appendix.

having it all:
why stop short of
the miracle?

Having it all requires changing your life by changing your unconscious or negative choices to conscious, positive choices. The formula for having it all has nothing to do with having a boyfriend, a husband, a baby, the right clothes, or the right hair, however. What it does mean is having your act together so that when you choose to have a boyfriend, a husband, a baby, or a certain look, you make positive choices that are proactive and correct in terms of the life your soul needs to lead. How can you know what these positive choices are? That is indeed the question. Because up until now I'm sure you thought that the choices you've been making *were* the best for you, otherwise, you wouldn't have made them. Nonetheless, as you discovered while answering the questions in the last chapter, when we choose from our head and not our heart, we abandon our path to a miracle. In order to begin making the choices that genuinely serve you, it's important to understand fully the parts of your life that are broken. With that thought in mind, it's now time to survey the anatomy of the rainbow in relationship to the anatomy of your own life.

know thyself

Let's look at each color of the rainbow along with the set of issues connected to it.

self-reliance

The first color of the rainbow, red, determines the difference between being a person who positively feels he or she is an "I have" as opposed to being a "have not." What is it that you need to have? First, you need to have a code of ethics that keeps order in your life and your community. You need to have abundance, the feeling that our material needs have been met. You need to have stability, the feeling that your professional and personal lives are in good working order. You need to have balance, to not feel overly submissive or overtly aggressive. And lastly, you need security, knowing that your bills are paid, that your environment is safe, and that you feel no sense of betrayal in your relationships. Those people who have the best sense of "I have" can often attribute their strength to a strong family unit that provided healthy roots. Those people who feel like "have nots," regardless of what material wealth they might have had, more than likely were deprived of a healthy family unit that provided stability, security, balance, and a code of ethics.

self-care

The second color of the rainbow, orange, determines the difference between being a positive person who is genuinely "happy" and feels good versus a negative person who is "sad" and feels bad. What do you need to feel happy and good? You need to feel pleasure, the feeling that your sexual needs are being met. You need to feel joy, the feeling that your days are filled with spontaneous laughter. You need to feel mobility, the feeling that you are not paralyzed or immobilized, and that your physical body is healthy and moving. You need to feel a sense of well-being, a feeling you get when you are eating right, getting proper rest, and engaging in healthy habits. People who have the best sense of "I feel good" can usually attribute their happiness to being raised in a balanced environment where appropriate self-care and self-discipline were modeled. People who "feel sad" are more than likely a product of a family given to extreme emotions exacerbated by abuse and addictive or careless behavior.

self-worth

The third color of the rainbow, yellow, determines the difference between a positive "I can" person versus a negative "I cannot." What do you need to feel that you can do anything? You need to feel empowerment, that you live by your own choices and not the choices others make for you. You need to feel confidence, the feeling of knowing you are as good as the next guy, if not better. You need to feel informed, that you know the answers to the questions that may be asked. You need to feel a sense of achievement, that your hard work will somehow be recognized. Those people who have a great sense of "I can" may attribute their strength to strong mentors who encouraged them throughout life. Those people who feel as if they "cannot" do anything are usually the product of environments that were at best indifferent, at worst characterized by verbal abuse or total neglect.

self-love

The fourth color of the rainbow, green, determines the difference between being a positive "lover" and a negative "hater." What do you need to be a lover? You need a sense of peace, that you are in harmony with the world around you. You need to feel a sense of forgiveness, that people are allowed to make mistakes and that harboring resentment is negative. You need to feel compassion, that everyone deserves love. You need to feel generosity, that in giving you receive. Those people who have the best sense of "I love" can usually attribute their strength to a nurturing environment. People who feel like hating are usually those who at best have been invalidated and betrayed in their closest relationships or, at worst, physically or emotionally abused.

self-expression

The fifth color of the rainbow, blue, determines the difference between being a positive "I express" creative and communicative person versus being a negative "I repress," which results in silence, lack of originality, or hearsay, better known as gossip. What do you need to feel creativity and the ability to communicate? You need to feel sincerity, that your truth will always set you free. You need to feel willpower, that you can follow through on your plans and commitments. You need to feel creativity, that all ideas are good ideas. You need to feel responsibility, that law and order in your life will enhance law and order in the lives of others. Those who feel a strong sense of expression can usually attribute their strength to a family that encouraged a strong sense of self-expression and valued the contributions of each member. Those people who feel repressed are usually the product of a critical or repressive environment.

self-exploration

The sixth color of the rainbow, indigo, determines the difference between the positive person who is "the sage" and the negative person who is "the know-it-all." What do you need to be a sage? You need to see with your eyes closed, drawing on your deepest intuition. You need to see beyond reality, to imagine the unimaginable. You need to see your life as inspired, to believe you can change the world. Those people who have a great sense of "I see" can attribute their strength to a positive, open-minded environment that encouraged introspective time. Those people who see nothing beyond "what is" usually come from an environment that viewed life in terms of black and white and never acknowledged the value of a sixth sense.

selflessness

The seventh color of the rainbow, violet, determines the difference between being a positive force, "the saint" or a negative force, "the sinner." What do you need to feel like a saint? You need to feel a sense of surrender, that you can lose anything without losing yourself. You need to feel patience, that you are right on time, no matter what time it is. You need to feel safe, the realization that all is well and all is as it should be. You need to feel gratitude, that you are thankful for every breath you take, every good thing, every bad thing, and every thing. Those who have a strong sense of "I trust" can attribute their strength to an environment that promoted a great reverence for God. Those who have a strong sense of distrust are usually the product of an environment that taught little reverence for the self or the world around us.

You have now been familiarized with the anatomy of the rainbow. But where does your own life stand in terms of this colorful picture? Answering the questions posed in the following short quiz will help to give you an overview.

red

—

I have abundance; my material requirements are satisfied:

yes   no   sometimes

I have stability; I have strong family ties, good friendships, and committed relationships:

yes   no   sometimes

I have balance; I have tempered my aggressive male and passive female energies:

yes   no   sometimes

I have security; I have a good job, practice fiscal responsibility, and dwell in a safe environment:

yes   no   sometimes

I have ethics and a code of honor; I regard all things and all people as equal:

yes   no   sometimes

orange

I feel pleasure; I enjoy a healthy sexual outlook and I spend time doing little things that I enjoy:

yes   no   sometimes

I feel joy; I find laughter in each day and enjoy being silly:

yes   no   sometimes

I feel a sense of control; I am not controlled by any addictions:

yes   no   sometimes

I feel a great sense of well-being; I am fit, practice healthy habits, and tend to my appearance:

yes   no   sometimes

yellow

I know empowerment; I set the rules and boundaries in my life:

      yes   no   sometimes

I know confidence; I have an unshakable belief in myself:

      yes   no   sometimes

I know the answer; I am a well-informed individual:

      yes   no   sometimes

I know achievement; I am able to set and make my goals:

      yes   no   sometimes

green

<hr />

I love peace; I am a lover, not a fighter:
        yes   no   sometimes

I love forgiveness; I do not hold anger, resentment, or blame:
        yes   no   sometimes

I love compassion; I have love in my heart for all people:
        yes   no   sometimes

I love generosity; I would rather give than receive:
        yes   no   sometimes

blue

—

I express sincerity; I never lie or undermine others:

      yes   no   sometimes

I express willpower; I can make a commitment and stay with it:

      yes   no   sometimes

I express creativity; I express creativity in my personal and professional environments:

      yes   no   sometimes

I express myself verbally; I am not afraid to speak my truth:

      yes   no   sometimes

indigo

I see beyond; I am extremely intuitive:

      yes   no   sometimes

I see imaginatively; I am inventive:

      yes   no   sometimes

I see choices; I am decisive:

      yes   no   sometimes

I see my purpose; I lead an inspired life:

      yes   no   sometimes

violet

I trust surrender; I don't cling to anything or anyone:

    yes   no   sometimes

I trust in patience; I know time is my friend:

    yes   no   sometimes

I trust fate; I know God always delivers:

    yes   no   sometimes

I trust gratitude; I thank God for everything and everyone:

    yes   no   sometimes

If you have honestly answered yes to all these questions, perhaps this book will only serve as a touchstone for you. For those of you who, like me, have had to answer no or sometimes, even a few times, keep reading. Fulfilling the tenets of the rainbow is within your grasp. Nevertheless, the rainbow is mysterious and elusive. It can disappear and reappear at a moment's notice. Learning how to keep your rainbow constantly visible to you and to others is your next step.

your fuel:
positive energy
enables us,
negative energy
disables us

philosophy: *e = me*

Your journey up until this point has been fueled with positive energy, negative energy, or a little bit of both. Most of us, along the way, have had our series of ups and downs, but if you find that you are experiencing more downs than ups, it's time to take responsibility and ask yourself why.

In order to understand the answer to that question, you must first stop blaming the world, your parents, your friends, your ex-lovers, or anyone you feel ever did you wrong. It is essential that you forgive it all if you are to reclaim your power. As you know, this is often far more easily said than done. As you work toward this goal, it might help to bear the following in mind—you don't need to keep the relationship, or have the person close to you, in order to forgive. Forgiveness is a mental, not a physical, state—a positive energy. Consequently, from this day forward you need to understand energy and how it can work for you or against you.

Energy is all around us. It is at once the most pervasive and the most indefinable force in the universe. Everything in our universe generates energy—animals, plants, minerals, and even color are all composed of energy. Most important, we are pure energy. By our thoughts alone we are constantly transmitting our own unique energy field or aura.

You do not need to immerse yourself in arcane mysteries of ancient thought or physics to understand the concept of how the energy of other people and places works with or against our own energy fields. Instead, simply consider the following:

Why do you feel a charge when you first meet somebody you are attracted to? Why do you feel depleted of your energy after an encounter with a person you don't like? Why do you immediately feel better when you step out into nature? Why were people like Princess Diana and Mother Teresa able to inspire millions with their love and courage? These are examples of the energy fields of souls who shape the way we feel about ourselves and the world.

Our energy fields need to travel in very specific directions in order to fulfill our divine destiny. We literally must learn to go with the flow and not against it. A simplified way of thinking about the flow of energy is what I call the Open Door Policy. It is, quite simply, the difference between trying to travel through a door that is open versus one that is closed. We are instinctively attracted to positive energy, as we are to colorful sunsets and open spaces. But often instead of following our instinct to pursue the positive and move toward the doors that are open to us, we follow our fear and insecurity, which lead us not only to doors that are locked but to dark corners inhabited by other people who have lost their way. And eventually we become used to these corners and call them home, despite their inherent negativity. It is this negative energy that gets us caught in recurring ruts of monotonous, unfulfilling work routines, perpetually unsatisfying relationships, and unsupportive, negative friendships. If we had traveled through the doors that were open, however, we could have avoided these situations completely.

The fluid motion of going through a door that is open is not unlike that of a stream flowing down a mountain. Our positive energy is not meant to be stopped. Its course can, however, be redirected when it faces an obstacle, such as a dam or a rock or, in our case, a negative person or situation. It is solely our responsibility to keep our stream as free and unsullied as possible by going around our obstacles rather than merging with them. When we fail to do this, the energy that once made us openhearted and joyful makes us closed-minded and distressed. Often only a thin line separates the positive energy that allows for creative communication from the negative energy that creates malicious gossip, or the positive energy of the wise and intuitive from the negative energy of the intellectually arrogant and ungraciously self-righteous.

Be warned that when we deliberately try to alter the flow of energy by enveloping obstacles or attempting to open closed doors, we go against the will of God. We begin forcing open doors that should remain closed and ignore the fundamental law of synchronicity. Instead of allowing things to fall into place, we attempt to manipulate circumstances. Before we know it, negativity is knocking on that door we forced open, prepared to teach us a painful lesson—a lesson that is often prolonged by the stubbornness that says, "Well, now that I've *got* the door open . . ." Remember, there is peace in surrender.

This is why children have such a simple but profound message to teach us. Children are the only people who by nature search for the open door rather than remain in the room. They instinctively stay out of their own way, because they have an innate ability to go with the flow of synchronicity. They follow the yellow brick road, never questioning the steps.

Why must it take us an entire lifetime to realize that the shortest distance between two points is a straight line? The straight line can be summed up in one thought: The path of least resistance has nothing to do with the hard road.

This is not to say that the path of least resistance will seem like the easy way—but the point is, it will only be difficult because *we* are making it so. We make it difficult when we resist it. And when you are having trouble distinguishing the path of least resistance, remember, it is the one that never leaves you feeling unsettled or unsafe.

In the same way, positive energy never depletes us of our

energy—it's always easy, it always falls into place, it always makes us feel good, and, most important, it strengthens our energy field, therefore empowering us. How can you be sure you are generating this positive energy? It's as simple—and as difficult—as changing the way you think.

philosophy: you are what you believe

Traditional scientific and medical thinking, in its preference for investigating only phenomena that can be reduced to precise measurements and categories, has never accepted the ancient ideas about the unquantifiable forces of energy. Yet this attitude is changing. The evidence is increasingly undeniable, for example, that our emotions and thought patterns generate physical symptoms; we know, and doctors now acknowledge, that by thought alone we can make ourselves extremely ill.

Many books have been written about the power of mind over matter. One of the better ones is *The Power of Positive Thinking* by Norman Vincent Peale, which profoundly illustrates this concept. More recently, Neale Donald Walsch's book *Conversations with God* shows us how affirmations enable us to set our own stage. It discusses the danger of "wanting" or being a "wannabe" versus subscribing to the belief that we have already received what we want. This tendency will take the form of thoughts like "I *want* to be happy," versus "I *am* happy," "I *want* to be thin," versus "I *am* thin, "I *want* to be rich," versus "I *am* rich." As long as you want, you will want for the rest of your life.

But the very best book to read—one that drives home the power of affirmations—is Louise Hays' *Heal Your Life.* A gem, a must-have for any library.

To ensure that you become enabled, a set of affirmation cards for the sole purpose of retraining your "headtalk" are included in this book. Most of us, including myself, need to relearn the way we speak about ourselves and to ourselves. An empowering concept for you to remember is that "where the mind goes, the energy goes"; think negative, you get negative; think want, you have want; think positive, you get positive. Believe in miracles, and so it will be. (For further information, see "Your Traveling Essentials.")

the color of energy

Energy operates in terms of frequencies. The seven energy centers move upward from the root energy center to the crown energy center in terms of the rate of frequency vibration. Scientifically speaking, colors follow the same rules of wavelength vibration. We grow from the bottom up, and the seven energy centers do as well. Each color is delineated by the speed of its frequency; red holds the lowest frequency of the rainbow colors, while violet holds the highest. Thus, it should come as no surprise that ancient thinkers saw that the energy centers possess color correspondences. And the spectrum of colors that match the seven energy centers is that of the rainbow—red (root), orange (sacral), yellow (solar plexus), green (heart), blue (throat), indigo (brow), violet (crown).

As you will see in the following chapters, color has a direct and very significant impact on the way you think, feel, and connect with the world. If you are feeling deprived, a good dose of red in your world—through wallpaper, clothing, even food—can go a long way toward picking you up; it is no coincidence that young children are often dressed in the vibrant shades of red, representing the color of safety and security, while some priests and mystics wear the holy shades of violet. Many ancient cultures knew this and utilized color as a cue for healing. Practitioners in ancient Greece and Egypt tinted rooms particular colors to achieve desired effects on the infirm.

The goal of this book is to maximize your potential by infusing each center with positive energy, pure color. We need to understand that color is energy and energy is information, and information leads us to transformation. Therefore, color is a reliable cue. In fact, people who read auras acknowledge the way people's levels of energy translate into different colors at different intensities. Thus, a person who is exhibiting high levels of confidence will project an aura of an intensely yellow hue, since yellow is the color associated with issues of self-worth and personal power. And when the energy is in a state of imbalance, colors appear muddy or thin. In the case of yellow, too little yellow in the auric field signifies apathy, fatigue, and lack of self-respect.

Skeptical? Consider the following: Was it strictly a coincidence that Mother Teresa was always clothed in white? That when Oprah launched her motivational videotape *Make the Connection,* she was surrounded by beautiful shades of orange, the color of well-being? Better yet, consider the movie *The Color Purple,* which profoundly portrays the issues of faith and surrender.

And, finally, have you ever wondered why saints and saviors are portrayed with halos or light emanating from them? Could the ancients see something now invisible to the naked eye?

Color is all around us. From the blue of the sky and the water to the reds and oranges of the sunset, to the green of trees and the vibrant indigos, violets, and fuchsias of our flower fields, we cannot avoid colors and are constantly influenced and affected by their energy, consciously or not. Yet whether we tap into this is our choice, a reflection of our dreams and desires. Often as we develop into adults, we neglect the importance of color, forgetting its primary place in our life when we were children. Consequently we end up wearing black and white, and thinking in black and white, never realizing the wellspring of potential that lies within the energy of color and diversity.

But whatever we forget, the child certainly remembers. What child do you know of who says, "Mommy, Mommy, can I please wear the black jacket?" And when you scan a crowd of people, what is the first thing your eye falls on? It's the person with the most colorful outfit. We are attracted to color because, as mentioned before, we are instinctively attracted to positive energy, and color is positive energy.

It is my belief that the seven colors of the rainbow are our seven steps to finding the open door, and we must include them in our daily lives. The individual chapters on color will provide you with a section of color resources. The color resource page will help you to visually incorporate specific colors back into your environment through various sources. Now it is time for you to meet your traveling companion.

your traveling companion: taking the hand of your divine child

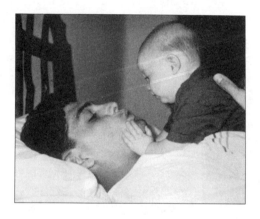

philosophy: "unless we become as little children, we cannot enter paradise."
—Matthew 18:3

The child has much to teach us—about the sense of wonder and infinite possibility, the capacity for forgiveness, the absence of judgment or self-doubt. It is clear to me that the child must be our companion and best friend as we navigate through the darkness of our days back into the light that is our birthright.

When we were young, we knew where we were going. We didn't need a road map, compass, or timepiece. The miraculous was our reality. We saw in Technicolor, and our thoughts embraced the infinite. Our needs were minimal and our hearts were infinitely receptive. As children, we saw things not only through innocent eyes but without limitations. Children know the ultimate religion of child consciousness: Bear no judgment. Seek joy.

Unfortunately, however, it is human nature to try to define things, and often things and people are defined with words such as ugly, old, bad, poor, strange, stupid. And it is not only these words but the accompanying actions that strip us of our inner spirit. Consequently, before we knew it, we had made a bargain with the world: Give me affection and recognition, and I will leave the sandbox, make myself over in your image, and conform to your expectations. Yet that original memory of paradise and oneness has not disappeared; it is simply underground, waiting to be recognized when we are ready to say yes to ourselves again.

The first step in reconnecting with your child involves creating a sacred space somewhere in your home that you can use daily for prayer or meditation. In order to make your inner child feel welcome, you might include a few items from your youth, such as a photo of yourself, locket, baseball card, work of art, or similar things. For example, the sacred space in my home encompasses a very small area on the floor that includes various colored rocks laid out in the shape of a heart. In the center of the heart I keep my childhood rosary, a small book of prayers, various feathers, and often small gifts or letters given to me by people whom I wish to pray for. To the right of my heart are three small candles I burn during my daily prayers. To the left of my heart are a few handmade Native American toys once loved by children from the late 1800s. These humble works of art are precious to me, for they remind me of the humility and sacred spirit that is so much a part of the Native American people. As you create your sacred space, don't be afraid to add items from other cultures, for regardless of how you create it, this area of your home will become empowered by each of your visits.

For those of you who want or need something less elaborate, a small photo of yourself as a child on a desk or near your bedside will do. As a sacred spirit there is no such thing as unsacred space. It can be as simple as closing your eyes and affirming the positive.

After you've claimed sacred space for yourself to allow for the child to emerge, you need to review where the child has been. Let's take a moment to look at the big picture of who we are and how we develop.

As mentioned before, God connects all the dots, and this becomes particularly apparent when we talk about the sevenfold nature of the rainbow and energy. Just consider: There are seven colors of the rainbow; there are seven days in a week; there are seven energy centers; and biblically speaking, it took seven days for God to create the universe. If you agree that life is energy, then it follows that the seven energy centers describe different stages in our life.

Recent advances in the study of biology have shown us that our body's cells renew themselves every seven years. The ancients intuitively understood this process, which they conceptualized in their description of the energy centers and the way we develop over our lifetime. Each energy center lines up with a seven-year stage in our life, and its central issues shape the way we develop during these periods. The progression from the red center to the violet center comprises all the challenges we must face on the road to self-enlightenment.

The following is a look at each one of these cycles and its connection to the themes of its corresponding energy center:

red

During the formative years from birth to age seven—the cycle of the red (root) center—issues of security, ethics, balance, and family will be especially significant. The degree to which these are resolved and dealt with in an appropriate manner will be of extreme importance later on in life. For example, a child of five whose parents divorce will not have had the best opportunity to experience positively the issues of stability and security that are critical to the root center. This lack of mastery of these issues will reappear later in life, when the adult has a difficult time maintaining stable relationships or financial security. A child not given a sound code of ethics is often a delinquent member of society.

orange

During the years eight to fourteen—the cycle of the orange (sacral) center—issues relating to self-control, pleasure, joy, well-being, and physical movement are paramount. During this cycle we learn to deal with our feelings, be they happy or sad, stable or volatile. If experienced positively, this is a time when we are able to stay positive and proactive and not get overwhelmed by our feelings. Those people who have difficulties in this period may find themselves easily depressed or moody. The years of the orange energy center are the salad days of childhood, when we bring our joyousness and lack of self-consciousness to bear on everything we do. It is the last stage before we must deal with challenging issues of identity and selfhood.

yellow

The yellow (solar plexus) center develops during the ages fifteen to twenty-one. Because these are the years when people establish a lasting sense of selfhood, issues relating to confidence and self-empowerment are particularly crucial. This is the time during which most people are immersed in high school and college and are acquiring the knowledge and skills to help them responsibly choose what career paths they will take. Here we meet the "in" crowd and the "out" crowd, those people who believe in us and push us to go to college and make something of ourselves. Those who are exposed to new information, encouraged to be creative and take chances, and made to feel self-confident will have a positive relationship with these primary third-center issues, and most likely succeed in life. On the other hand, those people who are not able to master such issues in this crucial period often end up lacking career skills and having a difficult time finding a comfortable identity in life. In a worst-case scenario, you find people who were pushed to perfection and were eventually pushed right over the edge.

green

While the yellow stage is a time when we tend to be more focused on empowering ourselves and establishing a strong sense of self, the years of the green (heart) center, ages twenty-two to twenty-eight, mark a period when we start seeing beyond ourselves and nurture our capacity for compassion, forgiveness, generosity, and love. It is a time when marriage becomes a consideration. Our ability to love ourselves takes on a new dimension here, because you have to have a strong sense of love for yourself before you can truly love another. For some it is a time when deeper emotional ties and/or families are established; others cultivate an environmental awareness of the need to reach out to the world around them. Either way, one cannot hold on to resentments if one is going to develop in this period. As previously mentioned, green is the middle and connecting color in the rainbow, the gateway to the second half of our development. Thus, it is a critical stage, one that determines how we find love and happiness in the later stages of our life and how open we are to spiritual issues.

blue

The years of the blue (throat) center, ages twenty-nine to thirty-five, are dominated by issues of self-expression, sincerity, creativity, and responsibility. It is the period when we finally find our voice (after all, blue corresponds to the throat center). If you have mastered the lessons of the previous stage, green, you have a deeper understanding of the imperatives of community; hence, your expression of your will—whether in your work, your creative endeavors, or your interpersonal communications—is done responsibly and lawfully. Not coincidentally, this is a period in people's lives when they firmly establish their career profile, or take it to the next level. Without a command of the lessons that the blue center offers, however, you can find yourself adrift in the world, personally and professionally, bereft of the willpower to bring dreams to fruition or to deal

with the obstacles holding you back. Our truth sets our course
and, over time, determines the outcome of our life.

indigo

The period of ages thirty-six to forty-two corresponds to the indigo center, when issues centered on the theme of self-explo-
ration—intuition, imagination, inspiration—are most central
to our lives. This is a swath of time when many people begin
their search for the clues that will provide their existence with
deeper significance. This, of course, is also the stage when the
notorious "midlife crisis" occurs for most people; often they
have established themselves in their careers, but still feel the
need to understand who they "really are." Many people do not
weather this period well. Either because they do not trust their
own intuition or are reluctant to indulge their imaginative ten-
dencies, they find themselves at a painful crossroads—work no
longer sustains them, but they are unable to see what else is out
there for them, or they make injudicious choices about what
will bring them fulfillment.

violet

The period from ages forty-three to forty-nine is the domain of
the violet center. This stage is, in one sense, the culmination of
the wisdom to be found throughout all the previous cycles, and
imparts to us the virtues that are essential for the second half
of our lives. It is a time marked by selflessness and surrender,
in which we learn to live with the experience of separation from
the world we have grown accustomed to. These are the years
when, among other things, we surrender parents and friends to
death; when many go through a divorce; or when children

leave home to attend college or establish their independence. When we have mastered this cycle, we are able to put our life in perspective. Our sense of self is so grounded, so deep, that we can afford to give it up, to trust in powers beyond ourselves, to effuse gratitude to God for the joy of being alive, and to be in constant pursuit of our deeper purpose. We have resolved many of the challenges of the preceding stages, from material security and professional stability to personal well-being and love, and are now prepared to make sense of it all.

Keep in mind that this model of the life cycles does not mean that a particular energy center is, or should remain, completely inactive during another energy center's cycle, or that you should pay no heed to the lessons of an energy center just because you are not living "in its time." As you work on yourself, try to think not only about how you relate to the issues dominant in your current life cycle but about the ways in which problems you are experiencing may have their roots in the inability to master the issues of previous cycles.

It is my hope that the above description of the ways to reconnect with your child and understand its development serve to reinforce one of the central messages of this book: that your inner child knows the way back home, and your child is smart enough to follow the rainbow to get back. Therefore, not only are you going to need to feed this child by utilizing the affirmation cards and the journal of questions found in this book; more than likely you're going to need to nurture and rear it once again. Using the seven colors of the rainbow, beginning with the lessons from the color red, you will give back to the child the colors that once belonged to him or her. It's time to believe again, and nobody knows how to do this better than the child within you. It's time to take the child's hand, for your child knows the way to the rainbow.

your traveling
essentials:
incorporating
mother nature

philosophy: we never stop needing mother nature.

Sorting out the negative people, places, and things is going to take time, and even a few tears. Therefore, it is vitally important that you take small steps to help yourself feel good and energized on a daily basis. There is no better helper than Mother Nature.

Mother Nature holds for us God's most powerful and awesome energy field. In her presence we are instantly renewed. Consider how you've felt if you've ever had the opportunity to swim in the ocean, hike through the mountains, or sail the high seas. I believe the closest we get to God while on earth is the high we experience when communing with nature. Unfortunately, however, most of us don't have the pleasure of being absorbed into the beautiful landscapes of Mother Nature every day. Nevertheless, there are simple ways in which we can bring Mother Nature back into our lives on a daily basis. For example, remember the expression "Cleanliness is next to godliness." With each shower or bath we can experience a form of baptism that renews our spirits and, for that moment, allows us to commune with our higher senses.

Mother Nature provides the four essentials of earth, wind, fire, and water, to help you to stay on course, allowing God's sacred gifts to empower you once again.

earth

Bring the outdoors in. Surround yourself with plants and flowers. They will heal you.

Sleep outdoors once in a blue moon.

wind/air

Open your window, let fresh air in to clear stagnant energy.
Spend time outside each day.
Practice deep breathing. A great technique is to visualize
that you are bringing in positive energy when you inhale
and expelling negative energy when you exhale.

fire/light

Keep your rooms well lit.
Open drapes.
Keep candles burning, even in the daytime.
Let the sun warm your face and body at least a few minutes
a day (wear sunblock to protect your skin).

water

Drink water. It will cleanse you. Eliminate soda, alcohol,
and coffee from your life.
Bathe at least once or twice a day to clear your energy field.
To aid you in this, philosophy, a personal wellness company, has created a special kit, the rainbow connection,
which contains seven highly pigmented, pure essential
bath oils that color and scent your bathwater and can be
used according to your needs and feelings. Also available
are seven highly pigmented bubble-bath oils for adults
and children. For more information call 1-800-LOVE-
151.

Along with Mother Nature, your traveling companion will
be grateful that you enhance your internal compass by stimulating the five common senses of sight, sound, touch, taste, and
smell, and the uncommon sense of intuition.

the common senses

sight: To energize your sense of sight, you must bring color back into your life in every way imaginable. Be creative! It doesn't have to be overwhelming to stimulate. Add colorful clothes, pillows, books, pictures, vases, etc., to your life.

sound: To energize your sense of hearing, bring music back into your life at home and at the office. The energy of music can excite or calm, depending on your needs.

touch: To energize your sense of touch, we recommend that you wear comfortable, breathable clothing. Nothing tight, preferably natural fibers. The key to your clothing from this point on is comfort, not conformity.

taste: To energize your taste, we recommend that you eat only the whole foods Mother Nature provides—fruit, vegetables, whole grains, soy products. If you choose to eat meat, fish, or poultry, make sure they are organic (nonchemically treated) and were raised in humane conditions (such as free-range chicken). Excessive junk food will impair your energy field.

smell: To energize your olfactory center, bring aromatherapy into your life with pure essential bath oils, candles, and diffusers.

the uncommon sense

intuition: Intuition is more than just the immediate feeling we carry with us at a particular moment. Intuition is God speaking to us. It is the internal intercom that constantly keeps us informed of both good and bad energy. It is the soft-spoken voice that directs us to the open door versus the closed door. And it is the voice that begins crying out with sounds of addiction, depression, compulsion, and obsession when we walk through the wrong door into the wrong space.

Most of us have forgotten how to use our critical sixth sense. Therefore, you are provided with twenty-eight affirmation cards (each with four issues for each of the seven colors) to facilitate your intuition. The important thing about using affirmation cards is that you never choose them—they choose you. Once the card chooses you, it demands not only that you pay attention to the issue at hand but that you affirm the positive in order to eliminate all negative energy. The affirmations serve a critical rule in reversing negativity and empowering positive energy once again. As we discussed in the last chapter, the universe supports positive affirmation just as readily as it responds to negative affirmation: Where the mind goes, the energy goes. An example would be if your intuition chose the color red for you one day:

color: **red**

issue: **security**

affirmations

i have security.

i have nourishment.

i have fullfillment.

i have contentment.

The core issue for red is "I have." If the issue your intuition wants you to work on is stability, the affirmation is not "I wish

I had stability," it is "I *have* stability." Remember, there's no room for questions or doubts when you're affirming. It is crucial that we remind ourselves that "I *have* stability; I *have* a clear path that I follow; I *have* the support I need; I *have* a relaxed life." (Feel free to elaborate on the infinite permutations of each affirmation. Thus, in the example above, you can remind yourself that you also have: a wonderful partner, a fulfilling job, supportive friends, a beautiful soul.) When we affirm the positive, we fuel ourselves with the positive energy needed for the spectacular journey that lies ahead. It's the most powerful form of prayer in existence. It affirms that what you are asking for has already been granted.

After the card has chosen you, it will steer you first to a page in the journal that will allow you to understand who you are by eliciting answers to questions that are pertinent to the particular issue. The purpose of the journal is to open you up, to remove the rock or the dam blocking the flow of your energy. And having these answers on record, in a journal you can come back to time and again, gives you a permanent record of your emotional and spiritual development.

When you are ready to begin the program, the affirmation cards at the back of the book can be used in one of two ways.

Linear: For those of you who are not used to relying strictly on your intuition as your guiding voice, we recommend that you go through the book from page one to the end addressing one color at a time, from red through violet.

Random: You can select a card at the start of each day and go through the corresponding section in the book for that card.

your daily prayers

philosophy: meditate.

It is my belief that when most of us wake, we feel renewed and rested. The morning is a wonderful time to reconnect our spirits with God. I believe the purpose of prayer or meditation is to celebrate "the present," God's moment. Therefore, although you can pray anytime in the day, I think it is important to be sure to put some time aside in the morning for your daily prayers or meditation. And while each of us will have distinctive ways we pray, for those of you who are not in the habit of praying, here are a few suggestions.

Begin by making yourself comfortable in your sacred space or wherever you are comfortable. Meditation positions include lying, sitting, standing, or moving. The key is to keep your spine straight and aligned. Next, recite a prayer or affirmation that resonates with you. Following is a prayer that resonates with me:

Dear God:

Heal me from the past. Save me from negativity and ill feelings. Release me of my ego. Forgive me for my sins. Allow me to forgive everything and everyone. Inspire me to show love to all that I come in contact with. Judge me not so that I will not judge others. Rescue me from those who wish me harm. Discipline me against slovenly behavior. Motivate me to play in your world. Help me help others. Strengthen me for the sake of my family, friends, and those who may need me. Guide me as only you can. Prepare me for your heavenly kingdom. Clear me. Relax me. Anoint me in your love. Baptize me in the purity of your spirit. Enter me and never leave. Hold me. Stay with me. Lead me. Love me.

Please help . . .
    (include prayers for others).

After reciting your prayer, it is my suggestion that you select one of the twenty-eight affirmation cards. As I have mentioned before, your affirmation card will choose you. Read the affirmation out loud or to yourself. You may add new affirmations if those printed on the card are not specific enough. Your next step involves holding one of those items from your childhood. I personally prefer a photo. You are now to look into the eyes of this child and either ask questions that are introspective, dealing with the feelings of this child, or you may ask more purposeful questions that deal with what the child may want to accomplish for that day.

introspective questions:

How do you feel today?

_____

_____

_____

_____

Why do you feel that way?

_____

_____

_____

Is there something you need me to do?

What is it?

How can I help you?

purposeful questions:

What would you like to do today?

What would you like to do for the world today?

What are you grateful for?

Whom or what would you like to pray for?

By creating a daily dialogue between yourself and your child, you put yourself in the present moment and provide yourself with inner guidance. This daily ritual will reaffirm your sacred path as your safest path in the world. But remember, if this is too much for you, prayer need not be complicated. It can be as simple as closing your eyes and affirming the positive.

your true colors:
how color
defines you

philosophy: we are all people of color.
without color we are colorless.

There is no question that as you begin to read the following chapters on color, many of you will begin to identify with a particular color. It may be your favorite color, or it may be the color that lines up with a particular trait with which you identify yourself. For example, you may be a writer, and so will naturally be drawn to blue, the color of creative communication; you may be someone who spends a lot of time doing volunteer work, so you will see yourself as a loving, compassionate green; or you may be someone with strong leadership and managerial skills, and whether you like yellow or not, the all-powerful yellow will be your dominant color.

It is crucial to remember that defining yourself as a particular color is not what *the rainbow connection* is about. Your goal is to find and balance the seven qualities inherent in the seven colors of the rainbow within yourself. In order to do this, you will need to define the people, places, and activities in your life that represent the traits of those individual colors. For example, you may find that although you view your father as an unloving person, without any green in his makeup, he is, nonetheless, a tremendous yellow who has imparted invaluable lessons about confidence and self-worth. Therefore, he becomes the color yellow in your rainbow. Honoring him as a strong yellow will shift a negative perception of him to a positive one and may then change the relationship because now you can see him for what he is rather than for what he is not. Perhaps your sister is a bit flighty, but always filled with joy and laughter; her contribution, then, is orange, not yellow.

To gain a quick perspective, refer to the following reference chart. Throughout, the key to building your rainbow connection is including a balance of each of the personality types in your world:

red = i have — ethics / family / balance / security
- a person whose priority is family
- a person who has gathered great wealth
- a person involved with keeping law and order
- a person involved in group or civic responsibilities
- social workers
- a person who provides essentials: transportation, the mail, military personnel

orange = i feel — pleasure / joy / control / sense of well-being
- athletes
- comedians
- psychologists
- psychiatrists
- physicians

yellow = i can — empowerment / self-esteem / information / achievement
- mentors, teachers
- entrepreneurs
- CEOs
- managers
- activists
- politicians

green = i love — peace / forgiveness /
compassion / generosity
  humanitarians
  environmentalists
  gardeners
  nurses
  farmers
  philanthropists
  caretakers
  healers/doctors
  personal assistants

blue = i express — sincerity / willpower /
creativity / communication
  lawyers
  actors
  aestheticians/stylists
  musicians
  public speakers
  writers

indigo = i see — intuition / imagination /
decisiveness / inspiration
  surgeons/diagnosticians
  visionaries
  sages
  movie directors
  visual artists: painters/sculptors
  scientists
  astronomers
  futurists
  philosophers

violet = i trust — surrender / patience / faith /
gratitude
    priests
    nuns
    rabbis
    monks
    pastors
    Zen masters
    Sufis
    lamas
    yogis

your destination: the house of miracles

philosophy: your spiritual family is with you for all eternity.

The benefit of filling your house with color is that you become the proud owner of a life not only guided by synchronicity, but of a life that is filled with purpose and fulfillment. The rainbow connection is not just about believing in miracles but about helping you discover the power to make them happen.

Ideally your rainbow connection will include all the people, places, and activities that bring positive energy into your life. As you work on your colors, you may recognize that being estranged from family or soul mate because they did not fit the ideal, were not a perfect rainbow, can be misguided. Hopefully you will acquire the skills to understand what other people's colors are, and to make sense of why they are a part of your life and how you can integrate them into your rainbow, not change theirs. The point of this program is not about someone else fulfilling the requirements of the rainbow, but about you fulfilling the requirements.

For those of you who are still searching for your true spiritual partner or soul mate, it is greatly to your benefit that you fulfill the tenets connected to the seven colors of the rainbow. If there is an absence of one or more of the seven qualities in yourself, you will more than likely attract someone who mirrors those voids, as we are often attracted to the people who fulfill a perceived lack in ourselves. The trouble with this, to borrow a phrase, is that two wrongs don't make a right. It's important to look for someone who complements you, not completes you. Hopefully, through this program, you will come to understand that if you need seven, you must be seven.

The following chart should help you to evaluate where you are in relation to the rainbow, show you how you may already be using colors to provide energy, and help you to think about which colors you need to enhance in order to complete your rainbow.

house of color

Red is the path of family, balance, ethics, and security. The life lesson is that "we are the world." The affirmation is "I have."

The people who are my red

_____

_____

_____

The places that give me red

_____

_____

_____

The things that are my red

_____

_____

_____

Orange is the path of pleasure, joy, control, and a sense of well-being. The life lesson is to "honor each other through pleasure and joy." The affirmation is "I feel."

The people who are my orange

_____

_____

_____

The places that give me orange

_____

_____

_____

The things that are my orange

_____

_____

_____

Yellow is the path of confidence, achievement, empowerment, and knowledge. The life lesson is to "honor yourself and your achievements." The affirmation is "I can."

The people who are my yellow

_____

_____

_____

The places that give me yellow

_____

_____

_____

The things that are my yellow

_____

_____

_____

Green is the path of compassion, generosity, love, and forgiveness. The life lesson is that "love is power." The affirmation is "I love."

The people who are my green

_____

_____

_____

The places that give me green

_____

_____

_____

The things that are my green

_____

_____

_____

Blue is the path of sincerity, communication, creativity, and commitment. The life lesson is that "truth shall set you free." The affirmation is "I express."

The people who are my blue

_____

_____

_____

The places that give me blue

_____

_____

_____

The things that are my blue

_____

_____

_____

Indigo is the person who follows the path of intuition, wisdom, discernment, and inspiration. The life lesson is "believing is seeing." The affirmation is "I see."

The people who are my indigo

_____

_____

_____

The places that give me indigo

_____

_____

_____

The things that are my indigo

_____

_____

_____

Violet is the person who follows the path of surrender, faith, patience, and gratitude. The life lesson is "I will, thy will." The affirmation is "I trust."

The people who are my violet

_____

_____

_____

The places that give me violet

_____

_____

_____

The things that are my violet

_____

_____

_____

part ii

seven steps
for making
miracles happen

You've been introduced to a new model for bringing positive, conscious energy into your life—the rainbow. You've learned that connecting with this energy involves confronting your fears, seeking out the spirit of your child, tapping in to the power of affirmations, and building your own sacred space.

Now you're ready to meet the individual colors that make up the rainbow, along with their particular emotional and spiritual issues, and see how you can incorporate them into your life or enhance their presence there. Since, as I've mentioned before, energy can flow just as easily in a negative direction as a positive one, you must learn to actively differentiate between these two poles. Consequently, we will look at the four central issues of each color in terms of both their positive and negative expressions and how your childhood might have influenced these expressions. Each chapter will give you a thumbnail sketch of how energy can get misdirected, and provide you with the tools to redirect the energy to the place you know it needs to go. Additionally, the following section provides you with a master chart entitled "The Anatomy of the Rainbow" to tell you where you fall positively and negatively.

As you work with the colors, strengthening your weak areas and spotting your blocked ones, try not to feel overwhelmed. You don't need to fix every issue at once. For example, perhaps you suffer from a thoroughly blocked orange; not only are you unable to motivate yourself to exercise, but you cannot create the time to pamper yourself, and you are so overworked and stressed that you can't see the humor in anything. Relax. Remember, this is not a race. Just work toward keeping your intention to move forward at the forefront of your consciousness and, over time, it will become greatly empowered, one issue at a time, and everything will fall into place.

The questionnaire at the end of each chapter, along with the journal section, will help you to target the source of your imbalance by breaking it down. It is my hope that this will help you to make better decisions about what you need to do to effect change in the future; in my experience when you isolate the things you need to do to break your bad habits, the task feels less overwhelming and you can begin to dissolve the blockages. I have also included a filled-out questionnaire for each color to help give you an idea of how other people have used them.

For example, you may find that you are still having a difficult time establishing your personal boundaries at work; your boss walks all over you and doesn't give you the respect you deserve. This would be evidence of a yellow center that continues to function disharmoniously. The questionnaire will help you isolate the factors that are contributing to a weakened sense of empowerment and focus on what you need to do to correct the situation. Also bear in mind that you can always return to the journal questions to help you clarify particular issues that are troubling you.

The most important thing to remember is not to become discouraged. The attention you pay to a blocked or broken energy center must be relentless—but the payoff is always there. It is no coincidence that many people's most broken energy center often becomes their best one. Consider Michael Jordan, who lost all confidence when he didn't make his high-school basketball team and yet went on to become one of the all-time greats! He is a wonderful example of a yellow who overcame obstacles to achieve the goals he had set for himself.

I have also included examples of completed "Major Break Questionnaires" on the next few pages so you'll have an idea of how to respond. When we are faced with a major crisis, it affects each of the seven energy centers. It is my hope that, as you read them, you will recognize the universality of many of these issues, and that you are not alone. I include them here because I feel it is important to know that a crisis requires a focus on seven of seven energy centers. Blank Major Questionnaires are included in the Appendices of the book, should you wish to examine a life situation more thoroughly once you have finished your color work. If that feels overwhelming, know that self-examination is one of the first steps toward reclaiming your self, your soul.

If, as you read these pages and do the work in each section, you find yourself debating whether or not the problems you face are ones you wish to tackle alone or with outside professional help, include God in your decision-making process. Many situations are serious and require some kind of professional intervention, particularly if there is abuse involved. In the event outside help is something you wish to investigate, a listing of self-help agencies is also provided in the Appendices.

Above all, be as honest with yourself as possible. It is that, and that alone, that will get you where you need to be—on the path of heart and soul.

a word about the color blue

There is a reason they call us "The Blue Planet." The issues associated with the color blue seem to cross over into every other color you will learn about. The color blue rules self-expression—dealing with our needs versus the needs of others. We *must* feel able to truthfully express ourselves verbally, creatively, responsibly, and with deep conviction.

Therefore, you can almost plan on working with blue issues for the rest of your life. The worst lies we tell are those we tell ourselves. The worst things we ever say are those things we tell ourselves but not others. The worst kind of willpower is when our power becomes the will of others. And the worst kind of responsibility is overresponsibility.

My purpose in telling you this is not to discourage you, but to give you hope. Knowing that this is something everyone struggles with has often given me the courage to speak the truth when I was most filled with fear. The lovely thing—the thing to remember—is that truth is contagious, and that "the truth shall set you free."

the major break: postponement

You can't move forward with two sets of baggage, yours and someone else's.

the color: all colors
my issues:

red: Abandonment—Fearful about losing my emotional support.

orange: Self-control—Not feeling in control of my life. Allowing others to take control.

yellow: Self-confidence—Feeling poorly about my image.

green: Forgiveness—Holding on to anger toward myself for being scared to confront things.

blue: Sincerity—Not being honest with myself.

indigo: Intuition—Ignoring intuitive feelings.

violet: Faith—Not trusting God to handle things.

the choice

What is the negative choice?

Staying in a long-distance relationship that is no longer manageable for me.

Why are you making this negative choice?

Because the person is an exceptional human being who loves me deeply.

What do you get out of making this negative choice?

I avoid being alone.
I avoid hurting someone.
I avoid making a hard decision.
I avoid revisiting the dating game.

What will you get out of breaking this negative choice?

A great sense of peace and freedom.
Relaxation.
No more stressful travel.
Better focus on the job at hand.
A nicer, kinder environment.
Control of my destiny.

Who or what supports you in this negative choice?

My deep need to love and be loved.

How does your past support this negative choice?

I felt abandoned as a child.

How is this negative choice postponing the life you wish to lead?

I feel unable to make travel plans.
I feel unable to get away from the rat race.
I feel unable to fully engage myself in my deep spiritual life.
I feel unable to maintain order and peace.

the change

In order to change you must acknowledge negative behavior and forgive. For the next thirty days focus daily meditation and/or prayer on the following affirmations. Deep breathing is extremely beneficial during this time.

I am willing to release the need to:
Hang on to situations or people because of my fear of abandonment.

I am willing to release and shed the past:
I am no longer angry at myself for postponing this difficult decision.

I am willing to release this pattern of negativity and avoidance of hard reality.
I am willing to release the negativity of a relationship that is working against me.

Forgiveness and reconciliation are two different concepts. Forgiveness is a must, reconciliation is optional. When you begin your forgiveness exercises, place your hands over your heart as you recite those things you forgive. Seeing yourself and those you are forgiving as small children will help you—it's so much easier to forgive a child than an adult. (If the person you need to forgive is deceased or you're having difficulty conjuring an image of him, try focusing on a photo.)

I forgive myself for:
Not turning things over to God.
Constantly trying to control the situation.
Not being honest with myself.
Being so hard on myself.
Not loving myself and for not taking better care of myself.

Being a coward.
The anger I feel toward both of my parents for their weaknesses.
Holding up my life.

I forgive my mother for:
  Allowing others to control her life.
  Being a victim.
  Always trying to influence my decisions.
  Her sadness.

I forgive my father for:
  Abandoning our needs.
  Being an angry person.
  Not bolstering my self-esteem.
  His inability to demonstrate his love and acceptance of me.
  Not always being honest.

the commitment
Never make a commitment you can't keep. Underpromise. Overdeliver. Don't seek perfection, seek a positive outcome.

the crawl
Begin daily affirmations of forgiveness and release.

the baby step
Seek professional counseling to help me make the break, if necessary.

the first step
Write a letter to my partner explaining my feelings and explaining that he should consider spending 50 percent of his time here because I can no longer handle the commute alone.

walking
Give the letter to my partner and wait one to two weeks for a response.

running
Take a short vacation to a spa or a retreat.

taking flight
Prepare for a new life with or without him.

affirmations
Love yourself. Believe in yourself. All is well.

the major break: denial

You can't move forward with two sets of baggage, yours and someone else's.

the color: all colors
my issues:

red: Abandonment—I never feel as if I have enough. I date only wealthy men.

orange: Self-control—My sense of well-being comes from feeling in control. Money helps.

yellow: Self-confidence—My self-worth always comes from the man I am dating.

green: Forgiveness—I am insanely jealous of other people/women.

blue: Sincerity—I used to be very creative. Now I do nothing. I lie constantly. I tell him I love him, but I really don't.

indigo: Intuition—I know I am ruining my life.

violet: Faith—I haven't prayed in years. God is not a part of my life.

the choice
What is the negative choice?
Staying in a relationship with a man I don't really love.

Why are you making this negative choice?
I want to get married so I don't have to worry anymore.

What do you get out of making this negative choice?
It gives me security.
I like knowing the bills are paid.
It makes me feel better than others because I have more.
I don't have to worry about working.

What will you get out of breaking this negative choice?
Freedom.
An opportunity to be with a man I really love.
Better sex.
A more honest existence.

Who or what supports you in this negative choice?
My need for material things.
My excessive need to spend.
My love for beautiful clothes.

How does your past support this negative choice?
I always felt poor, yet when I got new things I felt better, more important.

How is this negative choice postponing the life you wish to lead?

I'm selling myself short.

I'm selling out, and frankly I don't really have financial free-dom. I'm kept.

Freedom to really see what I can do on my own.

the change

In order to change you must acknowledge negative behavior and forgive. For the next thirty days focus daily meditation and/or prayer on the following affirmations. Deep breathing is extremely beneficial during this time.

I am willing to release the need to:
Hang on to a relationship just for financial security.

I am willing to release and shed the past:
I am willing to live with less.

I am willing to release this pattern of negativity:
By taking responsibility for myself. By exploring an employ-ment opportunity that could pay my bills.

I am willing to release the negativity of a relationship that is working against me.
I am willing to release the need to hang on to a man I don't really love.

Forgiveness and reconciliation are two different concepts. For-giveness is a must, reconciliation is optional. When you begin your forgiveness exercises, place your hands over your heart as you recite those things you forgive. Seeing yourself and those you are forgiving as small children will help you—it's so much easier to forgive a child than an adult. (If the person you need to forgive is deceased or you're having difficulty conjuring an image of him, try focusing on a photo.)

I forgive myself for:
Being greedy and hoarding my possessions.
Making money the most important thing in my life.
Using material things to bolster my self-esteem.
Stealing from others.
Being insanely jealous and paranoid about other people.
Constantly lying and pretending to be someone I am not.
Giving up a good job to be with a rich man.
Being financially irresponsible.
Not working.

I forgive my mother for:
Making me wear hand-me-downs.
Telling me to marry a rich man.
Selling herself out.
Living a lie with my father.
Being unhappy and uncomfortable with our financial status.

I forgive my father for:
Being a credit-card junkie.
Yelling at my mom for spending too much.
Not being a good provider.
Not telling me I was fantastic and wonderful.

the commitment
Never make a commitment you can't keep. Underpromise. Overdeliver. Don't seek perfection, seek a positive outcome.

the crawl
To affirm and forgive. To read a book on spirituality. To ask God for help.

the baby step
Get a job.

the first step
Start a savings account.

walking
Get an apartment.

running
If I find I only loved this man for his money, end the relationship.

taking flight
Date a guy I'm crazy about that isn't necessarily rich or poor.

affirmations
Love yourself. Believe in yourself. All is well.
> *I am rich.*
> *I have everything I need.*
> *I am successful.*
> *I have a good job.*
> *I have a beautiful place to live that I love.*
> *I can make it on my own.*
> *I will marry for love.*

the major break:
emotional abuse

You can't move forward with two sets of baggage, yours and someone else's.

color: all colors
my issues:

red: Abandonment—Fear of abandonment.

orange: Self-control—I feel very negative most of the time. I am used to giving up my control.

yellow: Self-confidence—I have very little self-worth.

green: Forgiveness—I have a deep need to feel loved. I love dramatics.

blue: Sincerity—I am afraid of expressing my true feelings.

indigo: Intuition—I see how ill my child is. I am unable to follow my intuition.

violet: Faith—I can't stop obsessing and worrying about how my child will manage without me.

the choice

What is the negative choice?

Putting my life on hold to meet the needs of my daughter, who is controlling and verbally abusive with me, her children, and her husband.

Why are you making this negative choice?

Because I love my daughter. I will never abandon her.

What do you get out of making this negative choice?

I get to take care of her children.

I earn money.
I have something to do.
I stay informed about her life.
I get to be a mother.
I stay in control, in a strange way.

What will you get out of breaking this negative choice?
Less stress.
Healthier relationships with my other children.
A healthier relationship with my spouse.
Peace.

Who or what supports you in this negative choice?
The money.
My daughter.
My need to be involved.

How does your past support this negative choice?
I had my brothers and sisters to take care of as a child.
I always felt responsible.
I was also a sickly child, so I am very sensitive to the needs of others.
Sadly, I think I like high drama.

How is this negative choice postponing the life you wish to lead?
I am missing a life of calm.

the change

In order to change you must acknowledge negative behavior and forgive. For the next thirty days focus daily meditation and/or prayer on the following affirmations. Deep breathing is extremely beneficial during this time.

I am willing to release the need to:
Take care of my forty-year-old daughter at any price.

I am willing to release and shed the past:
Of allowing my child to verbally abuse me.

I am willing to release this pattern of negativity:
As it is impairing my relationships with my other children.

I am willing to release the negativity of a relationship that is working against me.
I am willing to release the trap I built for myself.

Forgiveness and reconciliation are two different concepts. Forgiveness is a must, reconciliation is optional. When you begin your forgiveness exercises, place your hands over your heart as you recite those things you forgive. Seeing yourself and those you are forgiving as small children will help you—it's so much easier to forgive a child than an adult. (If the person you need to forgive is deceased or you're having difficulty conjuring an image of him, try focusing on a photo.)

I forgive myself for:
Quitting my job to work for my daughter.
Giving up all of my friends just to take care of her children.
Being so hard on myself.
Never saying no.
Allowing my daughter to verbally abuse me and her children.
Allowing my daughter to control my entire life.
Not setting boundaries.
Teaching my daughter the wrong values.
Taking money from my daughter.
Allowing my ex-husband to verbally abuse my daughter when he was angry.

I forgive my mother for:
Never telling me she loved me.
Never showing me she loved me.
Never telling me I was smart.
Telling me I couldn't go to college because I was a girl.
Sending my baby brother and sister to college.

I forgive my father for:
Allowing my mother to run the show.
Allowing my mother to scream at me.
Working too much.
Not being more verbally expressive.

I forgive my daughter for:
Her illness.
Being narcissistic and thinking only about herself.
Her verbal abuse to me and her children.
Her constant need for attention and control.
Using money to buy my obedience.
Her selfishness.

the commitment

Never make a commitment you can't keep. Underpromise. Overdeliver. Don't seek perfection, seek a positive outcome.

the crawl

Begin my affirmations. Pray to God for help. I need to be positive and strong.

the baby step

Make a list of how I've allowed people to walk all over me.

the first step
Seek professional counseling. I feel addicted to my need. I'm very afraid to let go or upset her.

walking
Make a list for my daughter of those things I will no longer tolerate. She must sign and agree to comply or I will not have a relationship with her.

running
If things do not change, I must leave. I must stop working for my daughter. I must not worry about her children. I must trust God to take over and pray for her healing.

taking flight
Accept my deserved retirement. Accept the unconditional financial support my other child has offered to me. Stay involved with my health club, tennis, and friends. Enroll part-time in art school.

affirmations
Love yourself. Believe in yourself. All is well.

I am loved.
I am talented.
I am a great artist.
I am worth it.
I deserve freedom.
I trust God to take care of my grandchildren.
I trust God to take care of my children.
I trust God to take care of me.
I deserve to be respected.
I am healthy.
I am happy and look forward to a happy life.

I am blessed.
I have great potential.

the major break:
physical abuse

You can't move forward with two sets of baggage, yours and someone else's.

color: all colors
my issues:

red: Abandonment—I am too afraid to leave for financial reasons.

orange: Self-control—I am extremely depressed.

yellow: Self-confidence—My self-worth is zero. Sometimes I believe I deserve to be hit.

green: Forgiveness—I hate him for hurting myself and my children.

blue: Sincerity—I am deathly afraid of saying what I really feel.

indigo: Intuition—My intuition is screaming that someone is going to be seriously injured.

violet: Faith—I don't trust God. He hasn't heard my prayers.

the choice

What is the negative choice?

Staying in an abusive relationship.

Why are you making this negative choice?

I am afraid to leave. I'm afraid he will take the children. I'm afraid he will kill me. I don't have the money to leave.

What do you get out of making this negative choice?
A husband.
A home.
A very false sense of security.
I can keep my family together.
I love my husband.
I don't want anyone else to have him.
I think he will get better.

What will you get out of breaking this negative choice?
I will no longer feel ashamed.
I will regain my self-esteem.
I will no longer live in fear of being hurt.
I may have a chance to find a man who will nurture me.

Who or what supports you in this negative choice?
My past; I was beaten as a child, and I expect to be hit. My children; they cry and beg me not to leave their father. They are very scared.

How does your past support this negative choice?
Same as above.

How is this negative choice postponing the life you wish to lead?
Every moment of my life feels fearful and negative. I long for peace and happiness.

the change

In order to change you must acknowledge negative behavior and forgive. For the next thirty days focus daily meditation and/or prayer on the following affirmations. Deep breathing is extremely beneficial during this time.

I am willing to release the need to:
Be beaten. To hold on to a person who is very sick.

I am willing to release and shed the past:
I am willing to release the pattern of abuse. I am willing to take back my power.

I am willing to release this pattern of negativity:
Of allowing him to ruin our lives.

I am willing to release the negativity of a relationship that is working against me.
I release the need for fear.

Forgiveness and reconciliation are two different concepts. Forgiveness is a must, reconciliation is optional. When you begin your forgiveness exercises, place your hands over your heart as you recite those things you forgive. Seeing yourself and those you are forgiving as small children will help you—it's so much easier to forgive a child than an adult. (If the person you need to forgive is deceased or you're having difficulty conjuring an image of him, try focusing on a photo.)

I forgive myself for:
Allowing myself to be abused.
Not protecting my children.
Knowingly choosing an abusive man.
Loving someone who is so ill.
Staying.
Giving up on myself.

I forgive my mother for:
Allowing my father to abuse me.

Not telling me she loved me.
Telling me I'd be just like her.
Giving me horrible advice.
Being a victim.

I forgive my father for:
His brutal beatings.
Never telling me he loved me.
Ignoring my every need.
His drinking.
His abusive treatment of my mother.

I forgive my husband for:
His illness.
His threats.
Permanently scarring my body.
His lies.

the commitment
Never make a commitment you can't keep. Underpromise. Overdeliver. Don't seek perfection, seek a positive outcome.

the crawl
Beginning daily affirmations and prayers. Turning my life over to God.

the baby step
Calling my local church or social agency for counseling and help.

the first step
Creating a task force of people or agencies who can help me make a break. Securing as much money as possible.

walking
Making an appointment with an attorney to secure a restraining order.

running
Arranging for a job and child care.

taking flight:
Getting my children and myself into a shelter.

affirmations
Love yourself. Believe in yourself. All is well.
> *I love myself.*
> *I will not allow myself to be beaten.*
> *I am safe.*
> *I am secure.*
> *God will take care of me and my children.*
> *God will open doors.*
> *I am loved.*
> *I am worth it.*

the anatomy of your rainbow

Take a moment now to consider the issues found within each color and their current manifestation in your world and your self. This can provide an interesting point of reference as your work progresses, and you change and grow. As you complete each step of your journey through each color chapter, return to this section and compare what you thought to what you discovered.

red: i have   positive   negative
ethics   _____   _____
family   _____   _____
balance   _____   _____
security   _____   _____

orange: i feel   positive   negative
pleasure   _____   _____
joy   _____   _____
control   _____   _____
well-being   _____   _____

yellow: i know   positive   negative
empowerment   _____   _____
self-esteem   _____   _____
information   _____   _____
achievement   _____   _____

green: i love   positive   negative
peace   _____   _____
forgiveness   _____   _____
compassion   _____   _____
generosity   _____   _____

blue: i express   positive   negative
sincerity
willpower
creativity
communication

indigo: i see   positive   negative
intuition
imagination
decisiveness
inspiration

violet: i trust   positive   negative
surrender
patience
faith
gratitude

red
self-reliance

philosophy: we are the world.

Red is the first color of the rainbow and is associated with our first spiritual energy center, which is located at our root, at the base of the spine in the perineum. The dominant energy center during the ages from birth to seven, our red energy center gives us our sense of belonging here on earth. It keeps us grounded in the world and gives us the energy to provide for our material needs and our family unit, and to live in harmony with the world around us. Red, the ultimate earth tone, demands that we honor the earth and all its species. There is no better demonstration of this thinking than the tribal and aboriginal religions whose trademark feature is the reverence for all of God's creations and the assigning of spiritual qualities to animate and inanimate entities. Father Sky, Mother Earth; animals as messengers, plants as healers; every rock, petal, blade of grass, and grain of sand is respected as an integral part of ourselves. We are reminded of red blood that flows through the veins of all living creatures. This is God speaking to us in color code to remind us that we are all connected and we must rely on one another if we are to survive.

As the first spiritual energy center of roots and foundations, red demands that you maintain abundance, stability, balance, and security in your life. When this center is functioning harmoniously, you feel connected to everything around you, and you have a secure and affirming attitude to the people and places that fill your world. When this center is not functioning harmoniously, you feel a deep sense of alienation from the world around you, which often includes family and friends. A deeply deficient red person is intent only on satisfying their personal needs and shows little regard for others.

If you follow the flow of red, you will never feel alone or out of sync with the world.

color: Red

location: Perineum (area midway between anus and genitals)

developmental years: 0–7

element: Earth

sense: Smell

physical organs: Bladder, blood, and circulation, bones and skeleton, colon, feet, hips, legs

the positive (the haves): Stability, security, safety, rootedness, commitment, ethics/order

the negative (the have-nots): Insecurity, frustration, restlessness, fear, separation, alienation, greed

archetypes: Colin Powell, Andrew Carnegie, our mothers, fathers, grandparents, sisters, brothers, co-workers, friends

conscious choices: Job security, safe environments, stable, committed relationships

your red resources

red aromatherapy: Rose, jasmine, cinnamon, cedarwood, clove, rosewood

red foods: Red peppers, red radishes, red potatoes, red apples, cherries, berries, red pears, pomegranates, strawberries, watermelon, raspberries

meditations and home life can be enhanced by red flowers: Roses, carnations, tulips

red gemstones: Agate, alexandrite, bloodstone, black onyx, garnet, smoky quartz, rose quartz, ruby

red rooms: The living room, the family room

red exercise and moving meditations
Music should be strong and rhythmical. Since movement should focus on the root chakra, at the base of your spine, use your feet, legs, and hips. Movements should be repetitious and rhythmic. Indian or African dance is ideal. Synchronize breathing to the music.

red movies and television (family issues)
> *Bambi*
> *The Sound of Music*
> *The Red Balloon*
> *The Red Pony*
> *The Swiss Family Robinson*
> *Amistad*
> *Schindler's List*
> *Dances with Wolves*

red books

The Family by John Bradshaw

Little Women by Louisa May Alcott

The Seven Habits of Highly Effective Families by Stephen Covey

The Seven Spiritual Laws for Parents by Deepak Chopra

The Gift of Fear by Gavin de Becher

How to Be a Perfect Stranger: A Guide to Etiquette in Other People's Religious Ceremonies, edited by Stuart M. Matlins and Arthur J. Magida. Volume 1. America's Largest Faith, Volume 2. Other Faith in America

affirmations

ethics

I have respect for all living things.

I have a code of honor.

I have integrity.

I have good principles.

family

I have healthy human relationships.

I have roots.

I have the support I need.

I have a sense of community.

I have stability.

balance

I have two feet on the ground.

I have balanced energy.

I have a connection to my male and female sides.

I have a feeling of belonging.

security
I have abundance.
I have safety.
I have nourishment and shelter.
I have concern for others' safety.
I have a connection to all living things.

family

philosophy: without roots, how do we grow?

the positive (stability, community)
You have two feet planted firmly on the ground. Your strong sense of stability can be summed up in one word—"family." A strong sense of family is one of the greatest gifts your parents gave you. It provides you with a critical piece to the puzzle of how to integrate well with friends, lovers, and your community. When this part of your emotional infrastructure is healthy and whole, you are able to feel a connection with others and, more important, you are able to keep your commitments.

the negative (alienation, separation)
You come from a house of pain. The family unit has been damaged due to divorce, death, or, even worse, abandonment, and your sense of family, community, and commitment is now impaired. Feelings of alienation and seperation in relationships of any kind can be overwhelming. You are prone to sabotaging relationships by either running away or clinging to people for dear life. Although it may not be your fault that your family roots were served, it is your responsibility to grow new roots.

conscious choices
Join a church or community group.

Work toward healthy parental and sibling relationships.
Adopt a family.
Pursue friendships and relationships with people who provide stability.
Work on being a good friend to all.

journal questions

What experiences from birth to age seven challenged your sense of family?

_____

_____

_____

_____

Who provides or has provided you with a strong emotional support system? How?

_____

_____

_____

_____

How do you deal with feelings of abandonment?

_____

_____

_____

_____

What can you do to lead a more stable and balanced life?

_____

_____

_____

_____

_____

security

philosophy: our roots bear trees, our trees bear shelter. without fertile roots the tree will bear nothing.

the positive (safety, structure, order, prosperity)
Your doors are locked, the bills are paid, and it is perfectly safe to be yourself. You grew up in an environment devoid of any physical or sexual abuse. More than likely, this environment was not critical or judgmental of you. This enables you to give and receive compliments easily. Wherever you go, your sense of structure and order keeps your anxiety level to a bare minimum.

As for prosperity, your cup is never empty, even when it's empty. You know you always have enough. Having money when you were growing up did not necessarily enable you to feel abundance, although it certainly helped. You learned abundance because you were taught that there is always enough to share with others, be it food, clothing, or shelter. Furthermore, your emotional and material needs were always met in a timely and reasonable way. No matter what, you are always willing to share with others, and, consequently, others are always willing to share with you.

the negative (fear, disorder, chaos, kleptomania, fiscal irresponsibility, cheapness)
You live by fear alone. At some point when you were growing up, your security was compromised; the people you trusted most betrayed your tender heart. When the doors weren't locked or your parents weren't watching, you got hurt. Or maybe they were the ones who hurt you; either way, it caused fear and insecurity. For others, insecurity was caused by excessive scrutiny and criticism, making you self-conscious about

your beauty, your brains, or your behavior. More than likely, this has caused you to be jealous and resentful of others. One thing is for certain: Wherever you go, you feel insecure and unsafe.

As for money, you grew up in a home where money or the nurturing of your emotional needs was scarce. There was never enough. Some of you couldn't get enough love, some of you couldn't get enough money, some couldn't get either. The result is an adult who, regrettably, operates in a self-involved, materialistic way and who constantly sees the glass as half full, never content with what you have. This is the root of the addictive tendency; you want more, but more is never enough. You spend money you don't have or penny-pinch to a fault.

conscious choices

Get rid of your credit cards.

Pay your bills.

Reduce your debt.

Keep yourself safe by locking your doors and wearing a seat belt.

Take a self-defense course.

Practice complimenting others.

Share your material possessions—your wealth, your meals, your home.

journal questions

What are your greatest fears? Who intimidates or frightens you?

_____

_____

_____

_____

_____

Whom or what have you lost in your life that has shaken your sense of security?

_____

_____

_____

_____

Do you enjoy giving compliments to others, or is this difficult for you? Why?

_____

_____

_____

_____

Whom or what must you have to make you feel secure?

_____

_____

_____

_____

How is your life impeded by fiscal irresponsibility or cheapness?

_____

_____

_____

_____

ethics

philosophy: with freedom comes responsibility

the positive (responsible, lawful, orderly, well-mannered, moral)

You are a law-abiding citizen who follows the rules. You have an inherent understanding that taking responsibility creates order in our lives and the lives of others. Your parents taught you everything from fiscal responsibility to social responsibility. You were allowed to spend your own money as long as you saved, too. You follow the speed limit, and you are a courteous driver. You clearly understand the consequences of not following the rules, because it only took you a few mistakes in your youth to figure out that the rewards were hardly worth the risks. As for your code of ethics, it is impeccable. You are moral, and you do your best to play fair with all people.

the negative (irresponsible, lawless, immoral, racist)
Remember the song "Call me Irresponsible"? You're an outlaw, more or less. You were brought up to survive any way you could. You stole when you had to, and if it was easy, you stole because it was easy. You cheated often, and if you didn't get caught, you cheated even more. You adjust the rules to fit your needs. You have a reckless approach to life. Concern for the welfare of others (and yourself) is not an issue for you. When you make mistakes, odds are you learn very little. Your modus operandi? You believe you are better than others and that the rules are for them, not for you. You have been described as a prejudiced person.

conscious choices
>   Stop cheating on your mate, your taxes, your tests, and yourself.
>   Stop speeding—you owe it to others, if not yourself, to keep the roads safe.
>   Don't even think about drinking and driving.
>   Follow the rules at work and at school, create rules in your own home.
>   Take on responsibilities at work or at home.

Be a person upon whom others can depend.
Commit to volunteer work if you want to understand the word "responsibility."

journal questions

Whom do you consider to be responsible? Why?

_____

_____

_____

_____

How would others describe your level of responsibility?

_____

_____

_____

_____

What are the root causes for irresponsibility in your life?

_____

_____

_____

_____

What specific actions can you take to be a more responsible person?

_____

_____

_____

_____

balance

philosophy: you are more secure
with two feet on the ground.

the positive (strong identity)
First there was Dick and Jane, then there was yin and yang, and now there is you. There is nothing nicer than growing up in a home where a balance exists between the positive qualities of nurturing and strength. Ideally, you were exposed to a balance of nurturing, gentleness, and receptivity and strength, courage, and loving discipline. Combined, they demonstrated to you your spear and your rose, so that you have blossomed and developed into a well-balanced individual who is neither overly weak nor overly strong.

the negative (extremes)
Me Tarzan, you Jane. Can you say "out of balance"? You're either a big bully or a passive pussycat. Whichever the case, there is an imbalance in you. You are much more in tune with one of the two sexes, able to relate to girls and not boys, or the other way around. This is not okay. You need to relate to and demonstrate a connection with both. Neither is more important than the other.

conscious activities
> Enhance your masculine energy through sports, martial arts, hiking, building, and taking leadership roles.
>
> Express your female energy by engaging in nurturing roles: caring for the young, assisting those in need—such as the elderly and the infirm—cooking, and gardening.
>
> Practice a standing meditation, instead of a sitting meditation for internal balance.
>
> Practice standing on a balance beam.

journal questions

Who do you feel embodies nurturing qualities/warrior qualities? Why do you like that aspect of these people?

_____

_____

_____

_____

Do you feel you embody more nurturing or warrior qualities? Why?

_____

_____

_____

Describe the people or situations that caused you to lose your balance, and why. Describe how you might change your reactions to them.

_____

_____

_____

_____

Describe ways in which you are too aggressive or too passive. How can you express yourself differently?

_____

_____

_____

_____

breaking it down now, to avoid a breakdown later:

it's time for a change

color: red
issue: financial

the choice

What is the negative choice?
Spending much more than I earn—too many bills—car insurance (sky-high from previous accidents).

Why are you making this negative choice?
To make myself feel better when I'm down or anxious. I feel too overwhelmed to do anything about my current situation.

What do you get out of making this negative choice?
Nothing. More problems.

What will you get out of breaking this negative choice?
Happiness, peace, and less stress.

Who or what supports you in this negative choice?
Extravagance—the need to be different.

How does your past support this negative choice?
My parents were always just working to survive.

How is this negative choice postponing the life you wish to lead?
I can't get into a new home. I want to go to cooking school for a career in cooking.

the change

In order to change you must acknowledge negative behavior and forgive. For the next thirty days focus daily meditation and/or prayer on the following affirmations. Deep breathing is extremely beneficial during this time.

I am willing to release the need to:
want better things than everybody else

I am willing to release and shed the past:
I am willing to stop spending on unnecessary things that caused my debt. By not wasting all of my money on fun and saving for the future, I will be happier in the long run.

I am willing to release this pattern of negativity:
of buying things I want versus buying things I need.

Forgiveness and reconciliation are two different concepts. Forgiveness is a must, reconciliation is optional. When you begin your forgiveness exercises, place your hands over your heart as you recite those things you forgive. Seeing yourself and those you are forgiving as small children will help you—it's so much easier to forgive a child than an adult. (If the person you need to forgive is deceased or you're having difficulty conjuring an image of him, try focusing on a photo.)

I forgive myself for:
Not pursing the goal of college.
Not doing better in high school.
Being a young, single parent.
Not getting into a career.
Not being happy and more social.
Not loving myself in a positive way.
Being so hard on myself.

Not liking myself.
Giving up.
Not believing in myself.

I forgive my mother for:
   Not encouraging me to do better.
   Not being able to show me more love.
   Not being able to give me things I thought I deserved.
   Not getting me a car.
   Not bettering herself in her field of business.

I forgive my father for:
   Not putting me through college.
   Not giving me more encouragement.
   Trying to show me love by getting expensive things for the family.
   Not following his dreams.
   Not working for his goals.

the commitment
Never make a commitment you can't keep. Under-promise. Overdeliver. Don't seek perfection, seek a positive outcome.

the crawl
Doing the release affirmations and forgiveness affirmations every-day until they are a part of me.

the baby step
Working with a professional to set up a budget.

the first step
Paying down credit cards to zero.

the walk
Setting up a savings account.

the run
Looking for part-time work as a cook.

the flight
Getting into a home. Giving my parents credit cards.

affirmations
Love yourself. Believe in yourself. All is well.
I have security.
I have my bills paid.
I have my family and friends.
I have order in my life.
I have talent.

breaking it down now, to avoid a breakdown later:

it's time for a change

color: _____

issue: _____

the choice

What is the negative choice?

_____

_____

_____

Why are you making this negative choice?

_____

_____

_____

What do you get out of making this negative choice?

_____

_____

_____

What will you get out of breaking this negative choice?

_____

_____

_____

Who or what supports you in this negative choice?

_____

_____

_____

How does your past support this negative choice?

_____

_____

_____

How is this negative choice postponing the life you wish to lead?

_____

_____

_____

the change

In order to change you must acknowledge negative behavior and forgive. For the next thirty days focus daily meditation and/or prayer on the following affirmations. Deep breathing is extremely beneficial during this time.

I am willing to release the need to:

_____

_____

_____

_____

I am willing to release and shed the past:

_____

_____

_____

_____

I am willing to release this pattern of negativity:

_____

_____

_____

_____

I am willing to release that which is negative for me:

_____

_____

_____

_____

_____

Forgiveness and reconciliation are two different concepts. Forgiveness is a must, reconciliation is optional. When you begin your forgiveness exercises, place your hands over your heart as you recite those things you forgive. Seeing yourself and those you are forgiving as small children will help you—it's so much easier to forgive a child than an adult. (If the person you need to forgive is deceased or you're having difficulty conjuring an image of him, try focusing on a photo.)

I forgive myself for:

_____

_____

_____

_____

I forgive my mother for:

_____

_____

_____

_____

I forgive my father for:

_____

_____

_____

_____

I forgive my _____ (other) for:

_____

_____

_____

_____

the commitment

Never make a commitment you can't keep. Underpromise.
Overdeliver. Don't seek perfection, seek a positive outcome.

the crawl

_____

_____

the baby step

_____

_____

the first step

_____

_____

walking

_____

_____

running

_____

_____

taking flight

_____

_____

affirmations

_____

_____

_____

_____

orange
self-care

philosophy: people can make you well, or people can make
you sick. choose wisely. choose consciously.

$f$eelings. So much of what we feel comes from our reactions to those around us. We let people bring us up, and we let people bring us down. Too often, we relinquish our happiness to another person's control. What we need to realize is that feeling good is an inside job, and it begins with caring for ourselves.

In our culture oranges have become synonymous with Vitamin C. Vitamin C is synonymous with feeling well. Feeling well is the epitome of positive energy and can only come from taking care of yourself physically, emotionally, and spiritually. No one can do it for you. When speaking of orange, God has provided us with a profound color cue. Orange also appears in our everyday environment through the primary energy source of fire. The ancients have long considered fire a great purifier for burning away negative energy. Furthermore, like a flame burning from a candle, God reminds us either to burn brightly or to risk burning out. And just as you must tend a fire if you want it to stay lit, you need to tend your inner flame with constancy and care. Not coincidentally, we light a candle in memory of a loved one to keep their spirit burning in our hearts.

Orange is the second color of the rainbow and is associated with our second energy center, which is located in the sacral area. The dominant energy center during the ages of eight to fourteen, the sacral center is directly concerned with our feelings of well-being, joy, pleasure, and abundance. It also influences our ability to experience sexual union as a spiritual activity that connects us to the life force through feelings of pleasure and well-being. This vital center keeps us attuned to the fact that feeling good physically means feeling good emotionally and spiritually. It is a simple idea that flies in the face of many spiritual traditions and religions, which view the cultivation of pleasure as a direct obstacle to the development of the mind or the spirit. According to those views, the body's pleasures are to be overcome, not attended to. Hinduism is one of the few religions that has adapted health and pleasure—through yoga, tantric sex, ayurvedic medicine, and sensible eating habits—as staples for everyday living.

When the orange energy center is functioning well, you have no problems connecting your physical health with your emotional health. There is plenty of laughter and physical movement, and you are comfortable with your body. When there is a blockage, there is addiction. Furthermore, you will have a difficult time experiencing the joy of life and the joy of sex.

The second energy center is truly the place where the mind-body connection is most clearly felt.

color: Orange

location: Lower abdomen to navel area; corresponds to sacrum area of the spine

developmental years: 8–14

element: Water

sense: Taste

physical organs: Kidney, reproductive system, spleen

the positive (the happy): Pleasure, joy, abundance, a sense of well-being the negative (the sad): Exhaustion, sadness, greed, depression

archetypes: Lucille Ball, Carol Burnett, Red Skelton, playmates, soul mates

conscious choices: Taking care of ourselves, regularly engaging in playful activities, including dancing, sports, hobbies, healthy sex

your orange resources

orange aromatherapy: Basil, galbanum, grapefruit, orange, ylang-ylang, geranium, jasmine, patchouli

orange foods: Carrots, squash, sweet potatoes, oranges, cantaloupe, kumquats

meditations and home life can be enhanced by
orange flowers: Birds of paradise, daylilies, or any other orange flower

orange gemstones: Amber, carnelian, coral, citron, jasper, topaz

orange room: The playroom, the gym, the bedroom

orange exercise and moving meditations
Music should be rhythmical or sensual. Latin music, such as the lambada, is highly recommended. Circular, sensual, and rotational movement of the hips and sacral area is recommended. Synchronize breathing to the music.

orange movies and television (laughter and feeling good)
Willy Wonka and the Chocolate Factory

Any comedies with Billy Crystal, Robin Williams, Jim Carrey, Richard Pryor, Mel Brooks, Steve Martin, Bill Cosby, Whoopi Goldberg, Eddie Murphy, Gilda Radner, Rosie O'Donnell, Tom Hanks
The Cartoon Network
The Comedy Channel

orange books (healing)

The Joy of Sex by Alex Comfort

You Can't Afford the Luxury of a Negative Thought by Peter McWilliams

The Five Elements of Self-Healing by Jason Elias and Katherine Ketcham

Make the Connection by Oprah Winfrey with Bob Greene

Spontaneous Healing by Andrew Weil, M.D.

Feeding the Hungry Heart by Geneen Roth

I Know Why the Caged Bird Sings by Maya Angelou

Heal Your Life by Louise Hay

Heal Your Body by Louise Hay

Bodywork by Thomas Claire

In the Meantime by Iyanla Vanzant

affirmations

pleasure

I feel pleasure when I pamper myself.
I feel pleasure during lovemaking.
I feel pleasure when I am touched.
I feel pleasure when I relax.

joy

I feel joy when I am able to let go of every detail.
I feel joy when I laugh.

I feel joy when I dance and sing.
I feel joy when I don't take life so seriously.

control
I feel good when I remain flexible.
I feel good when I move my body.
I feel good when I don't control others.
I feel good when I am in control of my own life.

sense of well-being
I feel a sense of well-being when I take good care of myself.
I feel a sense of well-being when I exercise and eat healthy foods.
I feel a sense of well-being when I look good and feel good.

pleasure

philosophy: feeling good is good for you

the positive (sensuality, ecstasy)
When you were growing up, your boundaries were wide but not inappropriate. Hugs were freely given and received. Laughing, playing, and experiencing your naked body in a healthy way was okay. You were told you were beautiful and that nothing about you was dirty. No one touched you inappropriately and no one beat you when you were bad. If you had questions about sex or "those special feelings," they were answered in a positive and un-threatening way. You take pleasure in all that you are.

the negative (masochism, rigidness, frigidity)
As a child, it was a cold, cold world. Hugs were nonexistent; perhaps you were even beaten when you were bad. When you were really bad you were really beaten. The messages about

your naked body or any other naked body were negative and "dirty." You didn't feel at ease with your body. Some of us may even have experienced the unthinkable—sexual abuse from a parent, relative, friend, or stranger. In the absence of professional help, the dots never did connect again. Consequently, most of your pleasurable experiences are often accompanied by an underlying feeling of sadness and guilt.

conscious choices

Engage in activities that you love: gardening, dancing, reading, painting . . .

Relax yourself by taking a long hot bath. Pay attention to the soothing effect the water has on your body.

Begin pampering your body properly with shower gels, scrubs, and body lotions.

Manicures and pedicures allow human touch to feel safe again.

Engage in gentle caressing with your partner.

Seek professional massage in a legitimate establishment.

Engage in healthy, uninhibited sex with one partner.

Seek professional therapy.

journal questions

What experiences during the ages from eight to fourteen might have affected your ability to experience pleasure fully?

_____

_____

_____

_____

_____

What specific activities give you pleasure?

_____

_____

Who gives you pleasure and how?

Describe one of the most pleasurable events of your life.

j o y

philosophy: laughter is medicine

the positive (laughter, enthusiasm, celebration)
The first pair of glasses your parents gave you were rose-colored. You take good, long, hard laughs at yourself often. You surround yourself with people who are caught up with joy, enthusiasm, and positive thinking. This allows you to take a bump in the road of life without incident. Your enthusiastic and optimistic outlook dries your tears and enables you to compose yourself; it serves as a constant reminder that it is essential to see the humor and goodness in all events.

the negative (negativity, pessimism, depression)
People who visited your home almost always felt exhausted. It was a place filled with sadness, depression, turmoil, defeat,

tears, and loads of negativity. There was little light in this place, as often the shades were pulled down and the curtains drawn. There was no way of looking at life in a happy way, let alone through rose-colored glasses. Over time, the cumulative effects of bad luck, things gone amok or constant negativity eventually beat you down, leaving you too depressed and weak to lift your spirits. It's the pit within the pit, where usually the only people you can find to join you are those who are just as down and out. The only laughing here is laughing at others.

conscious choices
See a funny movie.
Buy a book of jokes.
Set a goal of laughing at yourself at least once a day.
Surround yourself with upbeat people.
Smile more.

journal questions

What specific activities or people leave you feeling exhausted and depressed? Why?

_____

_____

_____

_____

_____

What specific things or people make you laugh?

_____

_____

_____

_____

How are you able to laugh at yourself?

_____

How can you bring more joy into your life?

control

philosophy: to want control is to be controlled

the positive (mobilization, independence, energy, flexibility)
You are a mover and a shaker. You do what you like whenever you like. Early on you learned the value of adventure, travel, bikes, roller skates, skis, trains, planes, and automobiles. Moving made you feel good because it made you feel happy, free, and alive. You are never afraid to make the next move in your life, because no one is ever there to tell you that you can't. More than likely your parents moved flexibly between appropriate permissiveness and discipline.

the negative (immobilization, addiction, laziness, inflexibility)
You came from one of three worlds:
   1. Your world never moved. Your parents would park themselves on the couch reading or watching television. If they did play, it was usually bridge or Scrabble. Naptime for either parent was a priority over playtime. As much as you might

have wanted to experience the joy of moving and playing outside, you were told to stay inside. Television or other miscellaneous indoor activities became habitual. Even moving furniture, not to mention moving to new neighborhoods, was an extremely rare event. The only thing that ever changed in your world was the weather, if you were lucky.

2. Your world was totally under control. Your parents were control freaks. They controlled the way you combed your hair, the way you brushed your teeth, the way you walked, the way you talked, the friends you kept, and, sadly, even your playthings. You are now a victim of either controlling others or being controlled. This lack of control set you up for life. As an adult, the moment you feel you are being even slightly controlled, you freak out. You either rebel by passively eating, drinking, drugging, or sleeping your life away or you aggressively begin to exert your control over others in an effort to get control of yourself.

3. Your world was always out of control. Discipline was completely absent from your life when you were growing up. Maybe your parents or guardians had to work all the time, so they were not around to give you the necessary guidance. Or maybe their own problems prevented them from controlling themselves. As a result, you lived by the seat of your pants. You did whatever felt right to you, never considering the consequences. Because of this upbringing, chaos reigns in your life by way of food, sex, drugs, or a combination thereof.

conscious choices
Take a walk or go for a bike ride.
Dance to your favorite music.
Stretch regularly.
Buy a trampoline.
Go swimming.
If resistant to exercise, get a buddy or hire a trainer.

Practice flexible thinking.

Make a list of how you are trying to control others.

Make a list of how you can feel less controlled by others and habits you have formed.

journal questions

What specific physical activities can you do to get moving again?

_____

_____

_____

_____

_____

Describe a situation in which you feel immobilized or controlled.

_____

_____

_____

_____

_____

Describe a situation in which you feel you are trying to control another person.

_____

_____

_____

_____

_____

What specific things can you do to release yourself from the addictions or emotions that control you?

_____

_____

_____

_____

sense of well-being

philosophy: a sense of well-being is the only state of being

the positive (health, happiness, beauty, self-discipline)
You are addicted to health. You were raised in an ideal setting where you were taught to eat right, get plenty of rest, and avoid cigarettes, alcohol, and drugs. Your parents led by example. It was an environment that stressed the value of self-discipline. But most important, every day was a good day in your household, because no matter how bad you felt, your parents made you believe there was no one more important, more special, luckier, or healthier than you. You knew all was well even when all was not at its best. It was a world wrapped up in positive feelings.

the negative (addiction, apathy, slovenliness, depression)
You are addicted to addiction. Every situation becomes a crisis. A sneeze is a cold. A tummyache is an ulcer. A bump on the head leaves you feeling poorly for days. Each problem is dealt with by introducing another one. Discomfort of any kind is treated with "medicine" (i.e., food, drugs, alcohol, spending money, sex) that numbs your senses. When you were growing up, your parents dealt with your bad behavior by depriving you of dinner or sweets. Good behavior got you lots of sweets that you didn't need. Your good deeds were rewarded not with genuine love and affection but with material items; in this sense, you were not unlike Pavlov's dog. But you learned always to want more, because more was never enough, and the addiction-to-addiction cycle began.

conscious choices

Keep a journal to get better in touch with your feelings.
Incorporate vitamins and a healthy diet into your life.
Be diligent and consistent with your daily grooming.
Practice relaxation techniques such as yoga or meditation.
Educate yourself about addiction; read books, articles, pro-
fessional journals.
Seek professional therapy.
Check yourself into a day spa.
Treat yourself to a manicure, pedicure, haircut, or massage.
Visit a doctor for a check-up.

journal questions

What specific events or activities help to give you a sense of
well-being?

_____

_____

_____

_____

_____

What specific events or activities have compromised your sense
of well-being?

_____

_____

_____

_____

Who are the people in your life that have made you feel completely cherished?

_____

_____

_____

What specific changes can you make to give yourself a better
sense of well-being?

_____

_____

_____

_____

_____

breaking it down now, to avoid a breakdown later:

it's time for a change

color: orange
issue: sense of well-being/control

the choice

What is the negative choice?

Not taking care of myself.

Why are you making this negative choice?

Habit and laziness. Feeling a lack of "control" in my life.

What do you get out of making this negative choice?

Indulgence. Ease. Postponement. An excuse for being de-pressed. An excuse for not moving. Ability to make excuses for how I look or feel. A way to create "physical" distance from others, i.e., padding or protection. Excuse for lack of control by being irrespon-sible for diet.

What will you get out of breaking this negative choice?

Self-esteem. Self-confidence. Energy. Beauty. Real control. Joy. Health. A better attitude. A more positive outlook. Freedom. A stronger desire to move my body because it feels better.

Who or what supports you in this negative choice?

Genetic history of overweight on both my mother's and father's side. Fast-food restaurants. Magazines and cover models.

How is this negative choice postponing the life you wish to lead?

I find myself avoiding opportunities to do certain things both personally and professionally. I find myself dressing in ways that are unattractive for me.

the change

In order to change you must acknowledge negative behavior and forgive. For the next thirty days focus daily meditation and/or prayer on the following affirmations. Deep breathing is extremely beneficial during this time.

I am willing to release the need to:

Be "invisible" from overweight.
Blend in.
Not be the best.
Isolate myself from others.
Be fearful of success or failure.
Stay overweight so I can make excuses for why I'm tired, why I'm dressing in "big clothes," why I'm pushing opportunities aside.

I am willing to release and shed the past:

Of thinking I need a perfect body instead of a healthy body. Of believing I will always have a weight problem.

I am willing to release this pattern of negativity:

I am willing to release my negative behavior by showing God my gratitude of being good to my body by taking care of my body and by moving my body.

I am willing to release that which is negative for me.

I am willing to release all the foods and things that are negative for my body.

Forgiveness and reconciliation are two different concepts. Forgiveness is a must, reconciliation is optional. When you begin your forgiveness exercises, place your hands over your heart as you recite those things you forgive. Seeing yourself and those you are forgiving as small children will help you—it's so much easier to forgive a child than an adult. (If the person you need to forgive is deceased or you're having difficulty conjuring an image of him, try focusing on a photo.)

I forgive myself for:
Letting my body go.
Not following through on my commitments to my diet and exercise.
Stretching out my skin.
The deep sense of disappointment I feel toward myself for not following through.
Not treating my health as a precious gift.
Postponing my life and missing great opportunities because I was too fat.

I forgive my mother for:
Her constant depression during my childhood.
Staying in her bed and not moving whenever she couldn't face her problems.
Teaching me avoidance.
Placing too much emphasis on my looks.
Teaching me to eat everything on my plate.
Calling me a "good eater."
Rewarding good behavior with food.

I forgive my father for:
Not helping me to have a better self-image.
Passing on the "fat" gene.
Using fat and food to avoid people and social situations.
Instilling in me the habit of overeating.

Not nurturing me more.
Not getting me the necessary help I needed when my weight be-
came out of control.

the commitment

Never make a commitment you can't keep. Underpromise.
Overdeliver. Don't seek perfection, seek a positive outcome.

the crawl

Doing my daily affirmations.

the baby step

Treating myself to an in-home massage once a week.

the first step

Following through on a three- to four-day per week one-hour work-
out including thirty minutes of cardio. Following a hygienic eating
program that excludes sugars, breads, pastas, and caffeine.
Emphasize fruits, vegetables, grains, water, and proteins.

walking

Begin exercising outdoors with a bike or hiking.

running

Take yoga one time per week.

taking flight

Join a team sport.

affirmations

Love yourself. Believe in yourself. All is well.
I am beautiful.

I am healthy.
I have a slender body.
I love myself.
I accept myself.
I love taking care of myself.
I love to move my body.
I love feeding my body things that are good for me.

breaking it down now, to avoid a breakdown later:

it's time for a change

color: _____

issue: _____

the choice

What is the negative choice?

_____

_____

_____

Why are you making this negative choice?

_____

_____

_____

What do you get out of making this negative choice?

_____

_____

_____

What will you get out of breaking this negative choice?

_____

_____

_____

Who or what supports you in this negative choice?

_____

_____

_____

How does your past support this negative choice?

_____

_____

_____

How is this negative choice postponing the life you wish to lead?

_____

_____

_____

the change

In order to change you must acknowledge negative behavior and forgive. For the next thirty days focus daily meditation and/or prayer on the following affirmations. Deep breathing is extremely beneficial during this time.

I am willing to release the need to:

_____

_____

_____

_____

I am willing to release and shed the past:

_____

_____

_____

_____

I am willing to release this pattern of negativity:

_____

_____

_____

_____

I am willing to release that which is negative for me:

_____

_____

_____

_____

Forgiveness and reconciliation are two different concepts. Forgiveness is a must, reconciliation is optional. When you begin your forgiveness exercises, place your hands over your heart as you recite those things you forgive. Seeing yourself and those you are forgiving as small children will help you—it's so much easier to forgive a child than an adult. (If the person you need to forgive is deceased or you're having difficulty conjuring an image of him, try focusing on a photo.)

I forgive myself for:

_____

_____

_____

_____

I forgive my mother for:

_____

_____

_____

_____

I forgive my father for:

_____

_____

_____

_____

I forgive my _____ (other) for:

_____

_____

_____

_____

the commitment

Never make a commitment you can't keep. Underpromise. Overdeliver. Don't seek perfection, seek a positive outcome.

the crawl

_____

_____

the baby step

_____

_____

the first step

_____

_____

walking

_____

_____

running

_____

_____

taking flight

_____

_____

affirmations

_____

_____

_____

_____

_____

yellow
self-worth

philosophy: there is power,
and then there is empowerment.

When we have self-worth, our life becomes a world of infinite possibilities. We learn self-worth from those people who act as guiding lights on our journey. God once again speaks to us in color code with the color yellow, the color of the sun. The sun lights our way through each of our days. The sun empowers our world by providing solar energy. The sun even empowers us by transferring its energy to plant life. This process is known as photosynthesis, and life could not survive without it. Without a doubt the sun allows us to grow anything within our world or within ourselves. Not surprisingly, a tactic that is often used to disempower prisoners is to cut them off from all light.

Yellow is the third color of the rainbow, the last of the earth tones, and is associated with our solar-plexus energy center, located in the abdomen, just below the sternum. It is most dominant during the ages from fifteen to twenty-one. The yellow energy center, like the sun, demands that we shine through to the world our knowledge, self-empowerment, confidence, and achievement. We can see the spirit of the yellow energy center demonstrated most profoundly in the Buddhist tradition, which emphasizes the pursuit of self-knowledge and insuperable self-discipline. It is no coincidence that their traditional garb is the color of saffron.

A healthy third energy center is the stuff of leaders: It enables you to be assertive without being overly aggressive; it gives you an indomitable sense of self-worth and dignity; and it ensures that you have the willpower to make your vision a reality. In our personal relationships, a harmoniously functioning third energy center ensures that you maintain the integrity of your personal boundaries through a strong identity. When this center is not healthy, you will feel your sense of self slipping away: You become wracked with self-doubt and the sense that you are not in control of yourself; eventually your identity is so porous that you become an easy target: someone of whom others can, and will, take advantage. You are the proverbial servant to the boss, or a slave to your need for perfection.

Yellow is a crucial stage in our path toward self-realization, where we come to understand that "I'm okay, whether or not you're okay."

color: Yellow

location: Below the sternum, extending down to the navel, just over the stomach

developmental years: 15–21

element: Fire

sense: Sight

physical organs: Gallbladder, liver, pancreas, small intestines, stomach

the positive (the winner): Positive sense of self-worth, confidence, empowerment, achievement

the negative (the loser): Negative sense of self-worth, lack of confidence, lack of control over life, fear of failure

archetypes: Itzhak Rabin, Indira Gandhi, Winston Churchill, Michael Jordan, Colin Powell, Muhammad Ali, César Chávez, Alan Greenspan, leaders, teachers, bosses, managers

conscious choices: Higher learning, leadership opportunities, self-assertiveness

your yellow resources

yellow aromatherapy: Grapefruit, lemon, tangerine, lemongrass, lemon balm

yellow foods: Corn, squash, yellow peppers, lemons, pears, grapefruits, bananas

meditations and home life can be enhanced by
yellow flowers: Freesia, yellow tulips, sunflowers, black-eyed susans

yellow gemstones: Apatite, calcite, yellow citron, tigereye, fool's gold, topaz

yellow room: The study

yellow exercise and moving meditations
Easy-listening or melodic music. Bending and turning of the solar plexus is recommended. Arms can swing side to side. Synchronize breathing to the music.

yellow movies and television
Hoosiers
Braveheart
Shine
The Mighty
He Got Game
Rocky
The Lion King

When We Were Kings
The Wizard of Oz
Yellow Jack
The Shawshank Redemption
The First Wives' Club
The Learning Channel
A&E "Biography"
PBS
The History Channel
Newshour with Jim Lehrer

yellow books

"No" Is a Complete Sentence by Megan Leboutillier
The Seven Spiritual Laws of Success by Deepak Chopra
I Could Do Anything If Only I Knew What It Was by Barbara
    Sher and Barbara Smith
Life Doesn't Frighten Me by Maya Angelou
The Seven Habits of Highly Effective People by Stephen Covey
Do What You Love, the Money Will Follow by Marcia Sinetar
Healing the Shame That Binds You by John Bradshaw
Women Who Run with the Wolves by Clarissa Pinkola Estés
Hope for the Flowers by Trina Paulus
Awakening the Giant Within by Anthony Robbins
You Can Make It Happen by Stedman Graham

affirmations

empowerment

I know I am worth all of the love and kindness the world
    has to offer.
I know that my presence here on earth is of great impor-
    tance.
I know better than to let people treat me poorly.

I know what my boundaries are, and I don't let people cross them.

self-esteem
I know I am the best I can be.
I know I am well liked.
I know I am a beautiful person.
I know I can do anything I put my mind to.

information
I know I am capable.
I know that knowledge is power.
I know I know the answer to the question.
I know and understand the world around me.

achievement
I know I can achieve great things.
I know that my work is a labor of love.
I know that I take pride in all that I do.

empowerment

philosophy: if you don't care about you, why should anyone else?

the positive (strong sense of boundaries)
You never draw first blood; when someone draws it from you, you stand your ground. Parents and teachers instilled in you the idea that you were capable of accomplishing anything you put your mind to. You have a strong sense of self and your personal boundaries. You do not allow people to treat you badly. People respect you because you respect yourself. Although you are highly responsible, you have clear boundaries about your level of responsibility for others.

the negative (doormat syndrome)

You suffer from the doormat syndrome. Your sense of self is so weak, and your boundaries so penetrable, that people walk all over you. More than likely, you grew up in an environment where your personal boundaries were not respected. On the other hand, when you were growing up, you might have had so little space to move around in that boundaries were unheard of. Some of you were subjected to bullying by a family member or a schoolmate. Because you were unable to say no, others took advantage of you. Now when you are challenged, you cave in. You hate confrontation—you would rather avoid it than get what you need and know you deserve. Not only do you never draw first blood—you're the blood bank of America!

conscious choices

> Make a list of how in the past people have disrespected your personal and professional boundaries, and how you could have handled these situations differently.
>
> Make a list of the things that intrude on your space, such as loud phones, television, or people, and what you can do to create an environment that respects your needs.
>
> Practice saying no.
>
> Stand up for yourself.
>
> Take a martial-arts course.

journal questions

What events or people have challenged your sense of self-worth or boundaries?

_____

_____

_____

_____

_____

Describe a person who you feel is tremendously empowered.

_____

_____

_____

_____

_____

What can you do to enhance your sense of self-worth?

_____

_____

_____

_____

_____

Describe a situation in which you felt totally empowered.

_____

_____

_____

_____

_____

self-worth

philosophy: baby, when you've got it, you don't have to
flaunt it, but you do have to know it

the positive (courage, confidence)
You believe in you. Your family and teachers taught you to feel
great about yourself, no matter what you did. You were never
told that you "didn't have it" even when it wasn't there 100 percent. You were encouraged to take chances with your brains,
and you were encouraged to be the best that you could be. You
were well liked because it was obvious to others that you liked
yourself in a healthy way. Anything they could do, you could
do, too.

the negative (shame, arrogance)

You believe in others because you were never taught to believe in yourself. When you were growing up, you were not allowed to make mistakes. You had to be perfect or you were considered a complete failure; but perfect was never perfect enough. You were often criticized, sometimes harshly, for everything from not knowing an answer to tying your shoes wrong, or simply for looking unattractive. Some of you were just ignored. You were not as well liked as you might have wished, because the more you were shamed, the more shy, defensive, or arrogant you became, and this alienated everyone around you. Any performances you had to give or tests you had to take filled you with anxiety, because the stakes seemed so impossibly high. Thus, you were easily psyched out and often choked. You believed you didn't know the answer before you were even asked. You believed you would be last to be chosen for a team, so eventually you stopped playing. You believed you wouldn't get the job or the date, so you eventually gave up and stopped trying.

conscious choices

Make a promise to stop judging others.
Make a promise not to criticize anything.
Read the biographies of leaders you admire.
Ask your boss for more challenging assignments.
Do something you're afraid of—it will greatly empower you.
Practice giving and receiving praise.

journal questions

What events or people have had a negative effect on your confidence?

_____

_____

Describe the feelings rejection evokes in you.

_____

_____

_____

_____

Describe things and people that make you feel more self-confident.

_____

_____

_____

What changes can you make in order to be more confident?

_____

_____

_____

_____

information

philosophy: knowledge is power

the positive (knowledge, power)
You are hooked on books. Reading isn't a hardship, it's a hobby.
You have expanded your horizons by expanding your mind. When
you were growing up, you were constantly exposed to new things,
and therefore developed a need for information. Learning was fun,

because it was made into an interactive activity; information didn't seem useless, so it didn't end up on the cutting-room floor of your mind. You easily apply what you learn to your life experiences. Furthermore, you feed your mind very little junk food.

the negative (ignorance, narrow-mindedness)

You haven't exercised your mind in years. You have always viewed learning as something that ended when you got out of school. Junk television is a staple. When you were growing up, C's were considered good grades—being average was perfectly okay. You were taken to "B" movies not "A" museums, and were never taught how to apply the information you learned. You didn't study because you were never taught how to study; you did only what was necessary to get by in school. You never developed a need to learn about the world "out there." Ultimately, you have limited yourself by limiting your abilities, and hence have settled for mediocrity in your life.

conscious choices

Read the newspaper daily, or a current-events periodical such as *Time* or *Newsweek.*

Watch only educational television.

Read the classics of world literature.

Plan one visit per month to a local museum.

Rent educational videos.

Learn a different language.

Go back to school for higher learning.

Travel to new places.

journal questions

What kinds of knowledge are important to you?

_____

_____

_____

_____

_____

What people or activities do not stimulate your intellect?

_____

_____

_____

What people do you admire for their intelligence?

_____

_____

_____

What kinds of knowledge can you acquire to empower your-self? How can you do this?

_____

_____

_____

_____

achievement

philosophy: a great leader is an equally great servant

the positive (success, leadership)
You follow your own heart and dreams, not those of others. You're a born leader. At an early age you were taught to set achievable goals and dream. You were blessed with mentors who had achieved and who had faith that you could also achieve. Best of all, they helped you to study, to get jobs, and

to look and feel your best. They taught you that your potential was unlimited and that if you didn't lead, someone else would. You understand that to lead is to serve.

the negative (failure, servitude)
You were written off at an early age and were fed the idea that "you'll never amount to anything" by your family, teachers, friends, and, later, your bosses. Your bar was set very low early on, and thus mediocrity has become the norm. Good mentors have been absent from your life, and your heroes growing up were either barely getting by or getting in trouble all the time. You believed that big dreams were unrealistic and that high achievement was for everyone else. Because you were unable to believe in yourself, you believed in other people, and willingly handed your power over to the people you believed in—and they were quite pleased that you did. Better not to try than to try and fail is now your guiding principle.

conscious choices
   Recite every day "What you believe is what you become."
   Dream big! And begin setting small, obtainable goals to help you believe in yourself.
   Allow yourself to make mistakes. Failure is a part of success.
   Eliminate all toxic people, environments, and habits that limit your ability to achieve.
   Read inspirational books.
   Find a mentor in your field.

journal questions

Which specific people have undermined your achievements?

_____

_____

Which specific people have assisted you in your achievements? What qualities in them would you like to emulate?

_____

_____

_____

_____

Which achievements are you most proud of?

_____

_____

_____

_____

What are your current goals and how can you achieve them?

_____

_____

_____

_____

breaking it down now, to avoid a breakdown later:

it's time for a change

color: yellow
issue: self-worth

the choice
We choose our life.

What is the negative choice?
Obsessive control and overcontrol of diet and exercise.

Why are you making this negative choice?
In my world of seemingly uncontrollable factors, this is the only thing I can have complete control over.

What do you get out of making this negative choice?
A false sense of order and calm. A great-looking body. A feeling that a "perfect" body makes me "perfect." My "own" thing as opposed to sharing something with friends or my husband.

What will you get from breaking away from this negative choice?
When I break it, I will get a feeling of guilt and un-balance, but in the long run I will be a healthier person.

Who or what supports you in this negative choice?
Society supports me by portraying the "perfect" image in the media. Casual friends support me by acknowledging

my results, complimenting me on my external appearance and dedication.

How does your past support this negative choice?
I was raised in a big, competitive, high-achieving, catholic family. "Love" was given not through hugs and kisses but with praise for your achievements. I always felt like I needed to be "perfect" to be loved by family and friends. When I was in my late teens and early twenties, I struggled with an eating disorder that resulted from the need to control something in my life and obtain this "perfect" image.

How is this negative choice postponing the life you wish to lead?
Everything ends up revolving around these two things, diet and exercise. I would like to live a life that is less restrictive. I want to feel a sense of accomplishment for who I am, not the ideal person I am always striving to be.

the change
In order to change you must acknowledge negative behavior and forgive. For the next thirty days focus daily meditation and/or prayer on the following affirmations. Deep breathing is extremely beneficial during this time.

I am willing to release the need to:
compulsively watch my diet and exercise routine.

I am willing to release and shed the past:
I want to do things because I want to do them, not because it is expected of me or because society tells me I should. I want to learn how to accept the positive results of a healthy lifestyle and not strive for perfection in image and performance.

I am willing to release this pattern of negativity:

I feel like I have been programmed by my upbringing to be the perfect daughter, the perfect wife, the perfect friend. I do what is expected of me, and I do it well. I tell myself my obsessive control of diet and exercise is the only thing I feel I do for myself, but in reality it is part of my striving toward a "perfect" life. I am willing to release that which is negative for me.

Forgiveness and reconciliation are two different concepts. Forgiveness is a must, reconciliation is optional. When you begin your forgiveness exercises, place your hands over your heart as you recite those things you forgive. Seeing yourself and those you are forgiving as small children will help you—it's so much easier to forgive a child than an adult. (If the person you need to forgive is deceased or you're having difficulty conjuring an image of him, try focusing on a photo.)

I forgive myself for:

Not being the best gymnast when I was younger.
Not being the prettiest girl in school.
Not being the most popular girl in school.
Not finishing college.
Having an eating disorder.
Having a bad day once in a while.
Not being a best friend to everyone.

I forgive my mother for:

Not teaching me about makeup or fashion when I was younger.
Not hugging and kissing me when I was growing up.
Not telling me she loved me until I finally told her I loved her.
Not being as strong and as independent as I wanted her to be.

Not putting trust in her own opinions, but worrying more about what I wanted to hear.

I forgive my father for:
Not participating and attending school and sports events while I was growing up.
Making me feel that love came with success and winning.
Not hugging and kissing me when I was growing up.
Not telling me he loved me until I finally told him I loved him.

the commitment

Never make a commitment you can't keep. Under-promise. Overdeliver. Don't seek perfection, seek a positive outcome.

the crawl

Taking a night off from working out without feeling guilty.

the baby step

Going out to dinner one night a week and eating whatever I want without feeling guilty.

the first step

Trying to avoid examining myself so critically in the mirror each day.

walking

Trying something fun and new without the nervousness of having to be the best.

running

working at making decisions based on my own feelings and not what I think others would have me do.

taking flight

Being proud of who I am. Living life with a freedom of choice without self-imposed limitations.

affirmations

I love myself.
I am beautiful.
I am perfect in every way.
I am making all of my own choices each and every day.
I am grateful for all that God has given me.

breaking it down now, to avoid a breakdown later:

it's time for a change

color: _____
issue: _____

the choice

What is the negative choice?

_____

_____

_____

Why are you making this negative choice?

_____

_____

_____

What do you get out of making this negative choice?

_____

_____

_____

What will you get out of breaking this negative choice?

_____

_____

_____

Who or what supports you in this negative choice?

_____

_____

_____

How is this negative choice postponing the life you wish to lead?

_____

_____

_____

the change

In order to change you must acknowledge negative behavior and forgive. For the next thirty days focus daily meditation and/or prayer on the following affirmations. Deep breathing is extremely beneficial during this time.

I am willing to release the need to:

_____

_____

_____

_____

I am willing to release and shed the past:

_____

_____

_____

_____

I am willing to release this pattern of negativity:

_____

_____

_____

_____

_____

I am willing to release that which is negative for me:

_____

_____

_____

_____

Forgiveness and reconciliation are two different concepts. Forgiveness is a must, reconciliation is optional. When you begin your forgiveness exercises, place your hands over your heart as you recite those things you forgive. Seeing yourself and those you are forgiving as small children will help you—it's so much easier to forgive a child than an adult. (If the person you need to forgive is deceased or you're having difficulty conjuring an image of him, try focusing on a photo.)

I forgive myself for:

_____

_____

_____

I forgive my mother for:

_____

_____

_____

I forgive my father for:

_____

_____

_____

_____

I forgive my _____ (other) for:

_____

_____

_____

_____

_____

the commitment

Never make a commitment you can't keep. Underpromise. Overdeliver. Don't seek perfection, seek a positive outcome.

the crawl

_____

_____

the baby step

_____

_____

the first step

_____

_____

walking

_____

_____

running

_____

_____

taking flight

---

affirmations

---

green
self-love

philosophy: love is power.

the best example of self-love is nature itself, because it is always giving, asking nothing in return. God has given us the color green as the dominant color in nature. When we see green, we are reminded of peace and tranquillity. Instantly we are transported to a greater reality. Not coincidentally, nature is called upon for the rehabilitation of young juvenile delinquents. There is no greater power than love, and we can all agree that we love nature.

Green is the fourth color of the rainbow and is associated with our fourth energy center, located at the heart. This energy center is dominant during the ages of twenty-two to twenty-eight. This critical center represents the middle space, where the energy of the earth centers (body) meets with that of the heavenly centers (spirit). The green center is related to the issues of love, compassion, forgiveness, and peace. It operates according to the idea that only love and empathy can ensure universal unity. We can draw an analogy between the issues of the heart-energy center and the Christian faith, which at its purest is based on the principles of love and forgiveness—"Love thine enemy," "Turn the other cheek."

When the heart-energy center is functioning harmoniously, you are at peace with your surroundings, because you are capable of forgiveness and empathy with those around you. If the heart-energy center is malfunctioning, you have a difficult time being comfortable in any environment, because your feelings of anger, resentment, and victimization run so deep. You experience the flip side of green: green with jealousy, green with envy, green (the color of money) that is considered a root of all evil, a gateway to greed. You cannot let go of these feelings and therefore are unable to receive the healing energy of forgiveness and compassion.

The heart center is the connector between the rainbow's lower red, orange, and yellow colors and its higher blue, indigo, and violet colors. Unlike the third center, it supports the desire to dedicate ourselves to others that turns "I" into "we."

color: Green

location: Heart

developmental years: 22–28

element: Air

sense: Touch

physical organs: Heart and lungs

the positive (the lover): Love, peace, harmony, compassion, generosity

the negative (the hater): Hatred, high drama, jealousy, mean-spiritedness, selfishness

archetypes: Princess Diana, Pope John Paul II, Oprah Winfrey, Louise Hay, Leo Buscaglia, parents, humanitarians, environmentalists, Good Samaritans, doctors, nurses, healers, farmers, caretakers

conscious choices: Making peace with your family, volunteering services, anonymous giving, environmental consciousness

your green resources

green aromatherapy: Eucalyptus, Norway spruce, pine, lilac

green foods: Grapes, kiwis, pears, green apples, limes, honeydew melons, peas, lettuce/greens, broccoli, celery, cabbage, spinach, parsley, herbs

meditations and home life can be enhanced by
green flowers: Gerbera daisies, bells of Ireland, St. Patrick tulips

green gemstones: Diamonds, emeralds, green calcite, jade, malachite, watermelon tourmaline

green rooms: The backyard, the bedroom, the garden/greenhouse, the children's room

green exercise and moving meditations
Music should be soothing, soft, and peaceful. Ambient and New Age music is particularly appropriate. Movement should include extending arms out and stretching up to open the rib cage or heart area. Large rotational swinging motions of the arms can be beneficial. Synchronize breathing to the music.

green movies and television
How Green Was My Valley
Forrest Gump
Beloved
Beauty and the Beast

Always
Driving Miss Daisy
Terms of Endearment
Casablanca
An Affair to Remember
It's a Wonderful Life
The Yearling
The Bridges of Madison County
Out of Africa
The Elephant Man
The Outdoor Channel

green books

Love Is Letting Go of Fear by Gerald Jampolsky
Why People Don't Heal and How They Can by Caroline Myss, Ph.D.
Return to Love by Marianne Williamson
Love in the Time of Cholera by Gabriel García Márquez
The Giving Tree by Shel Silverstein
Men Are from Mars, Women Are from Venus by John Gray

affirmations

peace

I love the peace I feel when communing with nature.
I love the peace and sanctity of my home.
I love the peace I feel when I detach myself from material things.
I love the peace I feel when I stop controlling others.

forgiveness

I love myself enough to forgive myself.
I love myself enough to forgive others.

I love the release forgiveness gives me.
I love being nonjudgmental.

compassion

I love who I am.
I love unconditionally.
I love helping others.
I love love.

generosity

I love giving to others.
I love being given to.
I love being generous in my everyday emotions, thoughts, and actions.

p e a c e

philosophy: to live in peace is to live in love

the positive (serenity, flexibility)

Like the trees, you bend. Your environment is gentle and calm. There is a time for play and a time for peace. As a child, you could lay your weary, tired bones into the lap of your mother or father and receive the silent affirmation that all was well through the soft strokes of tender, loving hands. Early on, you learned the necessity of going around an obstacle rather than meeting it head on. You know that conflict is never handled with more conflict; fires are put out with water, not more fire. You commune with nature often in order to feed your soul the kind of peace that no one else can provide. Like the color green, you operate comfortably between your earthly requirements and your spiritual needs.

the negative (drama, crisis, aggression)
You love a good fight. You've often been accused of being too aggressive or displaying manic behavior. When things go wrong, your response is always dramatic. You recall negative events in a catastrophic way. More than likely your environment when you were growing up was anything but peaceful. There was shouting and fighting; chaos reigned inside and outside your home. A walk in nature was a trip to the shopping mall. When personally affronted, you were taught to fight back; for some, it often didn't even take a confrontation to start a fight. Fighting was the norm and a learned behavior in order to get your way. You never learned how to be at peace with your environment because you never learned how to be at peace with yourself.

conscious choices
Learn how to interact with nature.
Listen to calming, beautiful music in your home or office.
When confronted with conflict, close your eyes and focus on your heart's response, not your head's.
Be as gentle with people as you would with a baby.
Learn to give in—it's okay.
Stop using foul or profane language.
Put down your dukes and start hugging instead.

journal questions

Who or what has had a negative effect on your ability to experience peace?

_____

_____

_____

_____

_____

Which specific environments or activities give you a sense of peace?

_____

_____

_____

_____

Who gives you a sense of peace? Why?

_____

_____

_____

_____

What can you do to bring more peace into your life?

_____

_____

_____

_____

forgiveness

philosophy: forgiving others is necessary, forgiving yourself
is essential

the positive (forgiveness, acceptance)
You live by the rule of forgiveness. You never hold on to anger
or resentment, and when you do, it's only for five minutes.
When you were growing up, you were allowed to make mistakes without automatically experiencing guilt or punishment.
In the highly evolved household, there was no need to forgive,
because forgiveness was assumed. Besides, your most important job was not forgiving, it was loving one another. Saying
you were sorry was the same as saying "I love you."

the negative (resentment, bitterness)

You learned that it was more important to be right than to be happy. Pride or ignorance, or both, would not allow you to open up and let the sunshine in. As far as you were concerned, everybody was out to do you harm. There is no room in your thinking for believing that people are fallible and make mistakes. In your mind, their mistakes are deliberate efforts to hurt you. The logic of payback motivates you. As for your parents, you forgive them the least, despite the fact that often they gave you the most. Even though they are the only parents you have, you punish them any way you can. You hold on to your bitter experiences of the past for dear life. Little do you know that if you would just let go of "it," "it" would let go of you, allowing for a lightness of being and happiness that could bring you internal peace once and for all.

conscious choices

Practice living in a state of acceptance. Call your parents and tell them how much you love and appreciate all they have done for you. Ask that they forgive your bad behavior. Make a list of all the important people in your life whom you have not forgiven. Call each one and release your anger by coming clean. Just say, "I'd rather be happy than be right. I don't want to hold on to this anymore."

To forgive a person who has passed away, write a letter to release your anger. When you feel you have unburdened yourself, dispose of the letter. Once and for all, let your feelings go.

If you find yourself forgiving the same person over and over, then maybe it's time to rethink your relationship.

journal questions

What does forgiveness mean to you?

_____

_____

_____

_____

_____

Who has forgiven you, and for what reason?

_____

_____

_____

_____

Whom have you had to forgive? Why?

_____

_____

_____

_____

Which people do you still need to forgive?

_____

_____

_____

_____

compassion

philosophy: if passion is the spark,
compassion is the flame

the positive (love, tolerance, caregiving)
Compassion teaches us to see all people as equal. You
have learned how to walk in other people's shoes and to be
kind, no matter what. You go out of your way for the less fortunate. You are able to feel another's pain without its becom-

ing your pain. Compassion helps us to understand that our goal must be not to condemn, but rather to redeem the finer qualities in people. The truly compassionate soul knows that we must feel compassion for even the most tortured and evil spirits.

the negative (mean-spiritedness, cruelty, codependency)
There is a good chance you are mean and cruel because others have been mean and cruel to you. The lessons you grew up with were "Fend for yourself"; "You're not my problem"; "You're bad, get away from me." You are accustomed to name-calling and laughing at people who are physically or emotionally impaired. You treat even the people you supposedly love in the same manner. Depending on the degree of condemnation you experienced growing up, your behavior ranges from that of a dog with a bad bite to that of a demonic monster. You never consider the effects of your behavior on others. On the flip side, you are someone who has taken compassion into the dangerous territory of codependency, for codependency is compassion taken to an extreme: It's love at any price.

conscious choices
Practice being a compassionate friend, lover, and family member.
Be sensitive to the needs of all people.
Always reserve a smile and a hello for your neighbors and the employees at frequented establishments.
Be more available for others.
Learn to be more giving to those who are less fortunate than you.
Do whatever you possibly can to help those who cannot help themselves.

journal questions

Describe a situation in which you needed compassion and did not receive it.

_____

_____

_____

_____

_____

Who has demonstrated compassion toward you? How?

_____

_____

_____

_____

In what specific ways do you demonstrate compassion in your life?

_____

_____

_____

_____

What specific things can you do to demonstrate compassion toward others and the world at large?

_____

_____

_____

_____

generosity

philosophy: it is a gift to be able to give

the positive (generosity, charity, hospitality)

Giving and receiving are synonymous, and the giver knows it. For you, giving is so much more than just giving money. It's giving of yourself, giving compliments, giving others a chance to shine. The essence of generosity is giving, doing the things with no thought of repayment and with no strings attached.

the negative (envy, jealousy, selfishness, pettiness)

You are green with envy or greed, and you love being a Scrooge. Hoarding and holding on are your mantras. You never go out of your way for anything or anyone. As for volunteering—it's for other people. Charity? What's that? You cannot give a compliment without feeling that you lose something, so you don't give any. Every time a friend succeeds, a piece of you dies. You are a confirmed cheapo who nickels-and-dimes everyone, even the poorest of people. Worse yet, you are cheap with everyone except yourself.

conscious choices

    Volunteer your services.

    Anonymously donate money to causes you believe in.

    Give a minimum of three compliments a day.

    Call the two people you are most jealous of and tell them how great you think they are.

    Share your material possessions—your wealth, your meals, your home.

    Share your friends with others.

    Share your time.

    Share your company with others.

    Share your parents with those who have no parents.

journal questions

Which people in your life are selfish with you? Why?

_____

_____

_____

_____

Who has recently expressed generosity toward you? How?

_____

_____

_____

_____

How do you express your generosity now?

_____

_____

_____

_____

What specific things can you do to become a more generous person?

_____

_____

_____

_____

_____

breaking it down now, to avoid a breakdown later:

it's time for a change

color: green (a combination of yellow-boundary and blue-over responsibility) issue: caretaking/guilt

the choice

What is the negative choice?

To help family members (by allowing my two brothers to live with me) without outlining or agreeing upon any conditions.

Why are you making this negative choice?

I believe that family should always help one another and because I felt the need to repay my "debt." My sense of responsibility and "I can do it myself" does not allow me to be comfortable owing anything to anyone.

What do you get out of making this negative choice?

Repayment of my debt. A sense of duty accomplished. The satisfaction of helping others. Built in baby-sitters for the dogs when I travel. The feeling of responsibility for holding the family unit together. Stress from a situation that has grown out of control. Anger over not being able to correct the problem for fear of creating discomfort in my own home and creating family problems. Hidden bitterness toward them for taking advantage of my generosity. Dismay and a feeling of failure for losing my own space.

What will you get out of breaking this negative choice?

A deep sense of joy and peace for regaining my space and my life. Oddly, it would seem I have more to lose than to gain. However, once I work through all the guilt, having a life of peace and joy is all I have ever wanted and that simplicity will make me truly happy.

Who or what supports you in this negative choice?

My irrational feelings of responsibility and, to some degree, my parents. Of course, the most support comes from my brothers.

How is this negative choice postponing the life you wish to lead?

I am only able to think of life as "when I have my own house I will be able to." I am curbing my social life and hindering the growth of my relationship by allowing myself to be a guest in my home.

the change

In order to change, you must acknowledge negative behavior and forgive.

I am willing to release the need to:

Feel solely responsible for my brothers.

I am willing to release and shed the past:

I want to live my own life. I want my own space to do with as I please. I want a life free from self-imposed feelings of responsibility of others. It's my life and I need to remind myself of that.

I am willing to release this pattern of negativity.

I am ready to learn the difference between care and re-

sponsibility. I am willing to accept the pain of change to gain personal happiness. I am braced to reinforce my own decisions and know they are not cruel or uncaring as others will try to make me believe.

I am willing to release that which is negative for me.

I am willing to learn less responsibility. I am willing to learn to protect my feelings. I am willing to face family confrontations. I am willing to learn and accept that every-one does not have the same sense of responsibility and that is okay. I am willing to learn to recognize manipulation, even if done unconsciously, and to learn how to not be taken in by it.

Forgiveness and reconciliation are two different concepts. Forgiveness is a must, reconciliation is optional. When you begin your forgiveness exercises, place your hands over your heart as you recite those things you forgive. Seeing yourself and those you are forgiving as small children will help you—it's so much easier to forgive a child than an adult. (If the person you need to forgive is deceased or you're having difficulty conjuring an image of him, try focusing on a photo.)

I forgive myself for:

Not being everything to everyone.

Feeling responsible for others' happiness in life.

Not wanting to become my mother. Even though it was an ideal childhood and I love her immensely, leading her life will not make me happy.

Expecting so much from others.

I forgive my mother for:

Being satisfied with a "Cleaver"-type family and not having her own identity.

Teaching me how to be a mediator and not create "waves."

Not taking responsibility for the family unit, now that we are adults, as she did in the past, as I feel she should.

I forgive my father for:

Teaching responsibility solely through punishment.

Not taking responsibility for his own life as I feel he should.

the commitment

Never make a commitment you can't keep. Underpromise. Overdeliver. Don't seek perfection, seek a positive outcome.

the crawl

Accept the situation as a challenge and formulate a timetable to initiate change.

the baby step

Start preparing the house to be sold.

the first step

Talk to my parents, accepting their feelings, but without it affecting my course of action.

walking

Talk to my brothers, expecting animosity and guilt trips, but accepting their feelings, and moving forward.

running

Let go of all guilt, feelings of failure, and feelings of responsibility so that I can start the next chapter of my life as a healthier person.

taking flight

start fresh, with a space that is my own, free from all the negative emotions and feelings.

affirmations

I am responsible for only myself.
I am a good person.
I am secure in my feelings and choices.
I am a better person for learning from new situations.
I am thankful for the opportunity to have choices.
I am healthy.
I am strong.
I can do whatever I put my mind to.

breaking it down now, to avoid a breakdown later:

it's time for a change

color:_____
issue: _____

the choice

What is the negative choice?
_____
_____
_____

Why are you making this negative choice?
_____
_____
_____

What do you get out of making this negative choice?
_____
_____
_____

What will you get out of breaking this negative choice?
_____
_____
_____

Who or what supports you in this negative choice?

_____

_____

_____

How is this negative choice postponing the life you wish to lead?

_____

_____

_____

the change

In order to change you must acknowledge negative behavior
and forgive. For the next thirty days focus daily meditation
and/or prayer on the following affirmations. Deep breathing is
extremely beneficial during this time.

I am willing to release the need to:

_____

_____

_____

_____

I am willing to release and shed the past:

_____

_____

_____

_____

I am willing to release this pattern of negativity:

_____

_____

_____

I am willing to release that which is negative for me:

_____

_____

_____

_____

Forgiveness and reconciliation are two different concepts. Forgiveness is a must, reconciliation is optional. When you begin your forgiveness exercises, place your hands over your heart as you recite those things you forgive. Seeing yourself and those you are forgiving as small children will help you—it's so much easier to forgive a child than an adult. (If the person you need to forgive is deceased or you're having difficulty conjuring an image of him, try focusing on a photo.)

I forgive myself for:

_____

_____

_____

I forgive my mother for:

_____

_____

_____

I forgive my father for:

_____

_____

_____

I forgive my _____ (other) for:

_____

_____

_____

_____

the commitment

Never make a commitment you can't keep. Under-promise. Overdeliver. Don't seek perfection, seek a positive outcome.

the crawl

_____

_____

the baby step

_____

_____

the first step

_____

_____

walking

_____

_____

running

_____

_____

taking flight

_____

_____

affirmations

_____

_____

_____

_____

_____

blue
self-expression

philosophy: Your life is a work of art—express yourself.

Self-expression just may be the most important aspect of our existence. Therefore, it is not a coincidence that God made blue the predominant color in our universe and that earth is known as the blue planet. Blue is the color of creativity, and no one would disagree that we are all part of the creative package or blueprint. When we experience blue, we see not only our blue skies but the deep-blue color of the ocean. Although all four elements are critical in clearing the energy field, water and air do so in a profound and lasting way that allows for self-expression. Blue is also used to describe a sad emotional state, and most artists would agree that pain is often the seed of great creativity.

Blue is the fifth color of the rainbow and is associated with our fifth energy center, which is located at the throat. This energy center is dominant during the years from twenty-nine to thirty-five. Concerned with the issues of sincerity, willpower, creativity, and responsibility, the blue energy center governs our ability to express our deepest thoughts and feelings in a truthful and lawful way. The Jewish faith offers a good example of a tradition based on obedience to principles of truth, law, and order: "He that keepeth the law, happy is he." The most obvious example of this is the Ten Commandments, which demand nothing less than our honesty, integrity, and honor. Coincidentally, blue is the color commonly associated with Judaism. Creative expression of our inner life is also a hallmark of the fifth energy center, and it usually takes the form of oral, written, and musical communication.

A healthy throat-energy center enables you to communicate your desires and intentions in a constructive and responsible way that respects the boundaries of others. It gives you the capacity to listen to your inner voice and find the tools to express it as truthfully and uniquely as possible. When this energy center is not functioning properly, you have difficulty translating your inner state for the outside world. Consequently, your communication with others is fraught with problems: You suffer from insincerity; or, you assert your own will regardless of the feelings of others; or you simply do not have the tools to tap in to your creative energy, and are reduced to mimicking others' ideas.

The lesson of the fifth energy center is that no one else can express your truth, let alone set you free.

color: Blue

location: Throat

developmental years: 29–35

element: Ether

sense: Hearing

physical organs: Mouth, teeth, throat, tongue, vocal cords

the positive (the communicator and the creator): Sincerity, willpower, creativity, responsibility

the negative (the gossip and the copycat): Gossip, codependence, imitation, lack of commitment

archetypes: Communicators such as Martin Luther King, Jr.,
Maya Angelou, Mario Cuomo, Ronald Reagan, Billy Graham,
great designers, musicians, actors, and writers involved in the
expressive arts

conscious choices: Telling the truth, acting responsibly, and
creating, creating, creating

your blue resources

blue aromatherapy: Jasmine, myrrh, olibanum, tuberose,
ylang-ylang, lavender

blue foods: Blueberries

meditations and home life can be enhanced by
blue flowers: Cornflowers, hydrangeas, lavender

blue gemstones: Aquamarine, lapis lazuli, sapphire, turquoise

blue room: The kitchen, the playroom, the crafts room

blue exercise and moving meditations
Soft flute or woodwind instrumental music is ideal. Drop head
down and use a gentle rhythmic motion of rolling your head
back and forth, side to side, and then all the way around to
open the throat area. Synchronize breathing to the music.

blue movies and television
Jerry McGuire
Dead Poets Society
Network

The Rainmaker
The Ten Commandments
Pinocchio
Good Will Hunting
Quality talk shows and news programming

blue books

The Artist's Way by Julia Cameron and Mark Bryan

A Creative Companion—How to Free Your Creative Spirit or any book by SARK

Watercolor for the Artistically Undiscovered by Thacher Hurd and John Cassidy

Write from the Heart: Unleashing the Power of Your Creativity by Hal Zina Bennett

Tongue Fu! by Sam Horn

The Ten Commandments by Laura Schlessinger and Stewart Vogel

affirmations

sincerity

I express sincerity in all that I say and do.
I express sincerity toward others.
I express sincerity regardless of the situation.
I express sincerity because truth is my guiding light.

willpower

I express willpower in all relationships.
I express willpower in defeating bad habits.
I express willpower in order to maintain my clarity.
I express willpower in order to set my intentions in motion.

creativity

I express my creativity in everyday life.
I express my creativity by writing down my ideas.
I express my creativity by doing things with my hands.
I express my creativity in charity and love.

communication

I express myself verbally.
I express myself through the written word.
I express my opinions even if they are unpopular.
I express myself without fear.

sincerity

philosophy: the truth will set you free

the positive (truth, honesty, integrity)

Your word is your bond. Keeping a commitment has never been a problem for you. Learning to tell the truth to others is fundamental; learning to tell the truth to yourself requires maturity and insight. You became a truth seeker because you came from an environment where telling the truth was rewarded and encouraged. There was little fear of being punished for making mistakes, be they deliberate or otherwise. The message was that you would be honored for your honesty and penalized for lying.

the negative (denial, deception)

Lying is learned behavior. You lie to cover up your shame and embarrassment for things you've done, things your parents have done, things you are, and things you are not. Some of us were taught to lie. "Tell them I'm not home." "Tell them the check is in the mail." "If you tell what I did, I'm going to hurt you." Yet another, and far more subtle, form of lying is the lying we do to ourselves. "I really love him," when you really don't. "I can stop drinking anytime I want to," when you binged last night. "I'm financially secure," when you're actually in debt up the wazoo. The very worst form of lying is the sociopathic behavior of twisting facts and reality to transfer your mistakes to others, altering the peace and serenity in others' lives by making them a part of your own dysfunction.

conscious choices

Make a list of all of the people you have lied to. If you can't call them and come clean, at least write down every lie you ever told and come clean on paper.

Be very conscious of your subtler forms of lying for a twenty-four-hour period. Make a note of every statement that was not necessarily true. "I worked all weekend." Reality: one hour. "I'll call you right back." Reality: two hours later. "I love your new haircut." Reality: You hate their haircut.

Ask those whom you love to bring your own insincerity to your attention.

Stop blaming others for your mistakes.

journal questions

Who has been insincere toward you? How?

_____

_____

_____

_____

How would you describe the sincerity of those you respect and admire?

_____

_____

_____

_____

_____

How do you think people would describe your sincerity?

_____

_____

_____

_____

How can you become a more sincere person?

_____

_____

_____

_____

willpower

the positive (focus, direction, discipline)

You can set a goal and apply the necessary discipline needed to achieve that goal. You operate best in disciplined, ordered, and structured surroundings. Your environment, although relaxed, requires that things are accomplished in a timely manner. More than likely, your parents taught you to use certain hours of the day to focus on the discipline required for learning. As for chores, you were taught to do your fair share. And messy rooms—unacceptable.

the negative (lazy, distracted, disordered)

Your life is out of focus. Things are constantly in flux for you. You have no regimen or schedule for anything. Life just happens for better or worse. Your home is messy, rooms are cluttered, and beds are often left unmade. There are no such things as chores or curfews for you. You do what you want when you want to. You don't aspire to hard work because being lazy is a lot easier. As for staying on a diet or breaking bad habits, you just don't have the discipline to do so, even though you'd like to.

conscious choices

Create a schedule for yourself at work and at home that includes time for play, studies, exercise, and meals.

Detoxify your entire environment by eliminating things you don't need. Learn to live with less.

Begin setting goals.

journal questions

How would you describe your willpower?

_____

_____

_____

_____

_____

How has a lack of willpower hurt you in the past?

_____

_____

_____

_____

_____

Whom do you admire for their willpower? Why?

_____

_____

_____

_____

_____

In what areas do you wish to improve your willpower?

_____

_____

_____

creativity

philosophy: you create your reality

the positive (creative, expressive, colorful)
Creativity is your compass and soul food. Blessed are the children who were raised in environments where creativity was encouraged. You were allowed to decorate your own room, dress yourself, style your own hair, and create meals. You were given crayons, paper, pencil, clay, cardboard boxes, pots, pans, and whatever else you needed to make your own kind of music and draw your own kinds of pictures. Best of all, when you sought approval for your work, not only were you complimented, you were encouraged to create more. Even today you bring creativity to every facet of your life, from cooking a meal to doing your makeup to writing a letter.

the negative (copycat, colorless)
Imitation is the limitation that has never allowed you to go higher. Your environment is sterile and stagnant. Music, crayons, paper, clay, and notepads are hard to find in your world. When you were growing up, you might not have been allowed to express your opinions comfortably, let alone your works of art. After a while you lost your voice, and your identity eventually became the identity of others. You took no chances, because it was easier to be and look like everyone else, instead of just daring to be different. You are an expert at writing form letters, following recipes, and coloring inside the lines. When you do create, too often you follow the blueprints of others.

conscious choices

Write in a journal.

Visit an art store and buy paper and crayons. Create something.

Make your own greeting cards.

Start a photo album.

Paint pottery at a local pottery store.

Write a letter or give a speech.

If you are computer literate, buy a graphics art program for your computer and play.

Bake a cake, but improvise on the recipe.

journal questions

What people or environments stifle your creativity?

_____

_____

_____

_____

Whom do you admire for their creativity? Why?

_____

_____

_____

_____

How do you like to express your creativity?

_____

_____

_____

_____

What specific actions can you take to allow your creativity to flow?

_____

_____

_____

_____

_____

communication

philosophy: talk, talk, talk

the positive (communication, expression)
You are a real talker. And better yet, you are a listener, too. You come from an environment of people who did an equal amount of talking and listening. You were constantly asked questions about what you liked, how your day was, what your thoughts were about world events, and what you would do to change things. You often sat down with a parent or a sibling just to chitchat. When you needed to be heard, you were always given undivided attention.

the negative (noncommunication, gossip)
These four ways of negatively communicating to others were all that were modeled in your home:

1. The gossip—Nothing nice ever comes out of your mouth. You are obsessed with talking about others in a judgmental or negative way. You embellish stories even when they need no embellishment.

2. The noncommunicator—You were told to shut up, shut your mouth, don't talk to me like that, etc., etc., etc. You have been verbally shut down, which has left you terrified to express yourself in the event that you may say something wrong.

3. The shouter—You had to scream to be heard. Your house was the loudest on the block. Your voice is now the loudest among your friends. You have been called obnoxious.

4. The dirty mouth—You need your mouth washed out with soap. If you didn't learn foul language from home, you learned it later on in life from your friends. You are using foul language either out of habit or because you really mean it. Either way, you need to change it.

conscious choices

If you are a gossip: Make a list of all the people you gossip about. Next to each name write something nice or don't write anything at all.

If you are a noncommunicator: During conversations with others, begin each sentence with how, what, when, where, why, or who to avoid getting yes-or-no answers from the people you're talking to.

Take singing lessons.

If you are a shouter: Practice using a soft voice.

Work on your listening skills.

If you are a dirty mouth: Eliminate one swear word per week. Create a penalty within the home or work environment, by which you pay a certain dollar amount for each swear word used.

Tape yourself saying these foul words and listen to how offensive and ignorant it sounds when replayed.

breaking it down now, to avoid a breakdown later:

its time for a change

color: blue
issue: truth

the choice

What is the negative choice?

The bad choice is lying or not being truthful.

Why are you making this negative choice?

One reason I'm making this choice is out of habit. Withholding truth is something I've done since I was a child. If I could lie well enough to deceive my parents, I could avoid being hit. Consequently, making this choice is part of who I am. Sometimes I don't even realize I'm doing it. The other reason I choose to withhold truth is to protect myself from confrontation or negative reactions from other people.

What do you get out of making this negative choice?

Protection. I can avoid situations and people that I may not wish to confront. Control. By choosing what you tell and don't tell others, you have more control over a given situation.

What will you get out of breaking this negative choice?

I've been actively pursuing the breaking of this bad choice for four years. I have yet to see the positive results of telling the truth. Being completely honest generates huge amounts of stress and sadness for me. I guess I can hope to attain more honest relationships with people. The other thing that seems to be an advantage is that you sometimes expedite the inevitable bad stuff if you tell the truth right away. It allows you to grow more rapidly.

Who or what supports you in this negative choice?

Everyone. Everyone is an unwilling supporter of this bad choice. Every time something goes well because I have withheld the truth, I get positive reinforcement. If you are good at withholding truth, no one knows you are doing it. It is a vicious cycle that only I can stop.

How is this negative choice postponing the life you wish to lead?

I want people to accept me for who I really am. If I don't show them who I am, they will never get the chance. I have seen people who walk their talk, and I admire them. Until I get my act together, I will continue with a negative self-image.

the change

In order to change you must acknowledge negative behavior and forgive. For the next thirty days focus daily meditation and/or prayer on the following affirmations. Deep breathing is extremely beneficial during this time.

I am willing to release the need to:

Avoid confrontation.

I am willing to release and shed the past:

Not being truthful is a pattern of behavior born of fear. I will try to release the past, because it can no longer hurt me.

I am willing to release this pattern of negativity:

Not being truthful causes its own kind of pain. It iso-

*lates you from everyone, including those who love you. I don't want to
be isolated.*

I am willing to release that which is negative for me:
 *confrontation appears to be a negative thing, to me. Not being
truthful is also negative for me. I'm willing to see confrontation as
a tool for growth, while freeing myself from the chains of deceit.*

Forgiveness and reconciliation are two different concepts. Forgiveness is a must, reconciliation is optional. When you begin
your forgiveness exercises, place your hands over your heart as
you recite those things you forgive. Seeing yourself and those
you are forgiving as small children will help you—it's so much
easier to forgive a child than an adult. (If the person you need
to forgive is deceased or you're having difficulty conjuring an
image of him, try focusing on a photo.)

I forgive myself for:
 *Hurting other people.
Not always being a good person.
Feeling anger and fear.*

I forgive my mother for:
 Not showing me that it's okay to feel every emotion.

I forgive my father for:
 *Making me feel insignificant.
Hitting me.
Humiliating me.*

the commitment
Never make a commitment you can't keep. Underpromise.
Overdeliver. Don't seek perfection, seek a positive outcome.

the crawl
Awareness. I would begin by making journal entries about situations in which I was not being truthful. This would give me an opportunity to recognize how often I make this choice.

the baby step
Role-playing. I could find someone I trust to discuss a situation where I was not being truthful. I would role-play that situation with my friend and actually say what I should have said to begin with.

the first step
Test the waters. If I catch myself not being truthful in a low-risk situation, I could stop and try to be more truthful in what I was saying. I would go back to my journal and keep a record of how many times I did this and what the outcome was.

walking
Go for it. If I could break myself of the impulse to not be truthful, I could then be more honest in high-risk situations. This would be the most difficult step for me, because it would require confrontation, which I hate. I would need a lot of reassurance from friends and family that even though there was pain involved in making a good choice, it is ultimately in my best interest.

taking flight

I don't know if I will ever reach this level. I think I might go back and confront people that I may have hurt by not being truthful. I would carefully assess whether or not it would be beneficial for both people.

affirmations

Love yourself. Believe in yourself. All is well.

The truth will set me free.

I am not afraid to tell the truth.

I am secure that honesty is the best policy.

your "work" sheet

breaking it down now, to avoid a breakdown later:

it's time for a change

color: _____
issue: _____

the choice

What is the negative choice?

_____
_____
_____

Why are you making this negative choice?

_____
_____
_____

What do you get out of making this negative choice?

_____
_____
_____

What will you get out of breaking this negative choice?

_____
_____
_____

Who or what supports you in this negative choice?

_____

_____

_____

How is this negative choice postponing the life you wish to lead?

_____

_____

_____

the change

In order to change you must acknowledge negative behavior and forgive. For the next thirty days focus daily meditation and/or prayer on the following affirmations. Deep breathing is extremely beneficial during this time.

I am willing to release the need to:

_____

_____

_____

_____

I am willing to release and shed the past:

_____

_____

_____

_____

I am willing to release this pattern of negativity:

_____

_____

_____

_____

I am willing to release that which is negative for me:

_____

_____

_____

_____

_____

Forgiveness and reconciliation are two different concepts. Forgiveness is a must, reconciliation is optional. When you begin your forgiveness exercises, place your hands over your heart as you recite those things you forgive. Seeing yourself and those you are forgiving as small children will help you—it's so much easier to forgive a child than an adult. (If the person you need to forgive is deceased or you're having difficulty conjuring an image of him, try focusing on a photo.)

I forgive myself for:

_____

_____

_____

_____

I forgive my mother for:

_____

_____

_____

_____

I forgive my father for:

_____

_____

_____

_____
_____
I forgive my _____ (other) for:

_____
_____
_____
_____
_____

the commitment
Never make a commitment you can't keep. Underpromise.
Overdeliver. Don't seek perfection, seek a positive outcome.

the crawl
_____
_____

the baby step
_____
_____

the first step
_____
_____

walking
_____
_____

running
_____
_____

taking flight

_____

_____

affirmations

_____

_____

_____

_____

_____

indigo
self-exploration

philosophy: believing is seeing.

Self-discovery can be experienced only during the quiet times of our days. Indigo, the color associated with self-discovery, is a color often absent from our visual field because indigo hides out, requiring its own quiet. When we view a variety of many different-colored flowers, we are often drawn into the indigo and violet shades as if we were listening to a song that we love but never hear enough of. The shade of indigo and even violet has long been associated with mystics and saints. Indigo demands exploration, bringing us inside and even underground in order to understand our deepest and most profound questions, those that can be answered only be the invisible world.

Indigo is the sixth color of the rainbow and is associated with our sixth energy center, located between the eyebrows and often referred to as the "third eye." The "third eye" or brow center is most dominant between the ages of thirty-six and forty-two. The sixth energy center is commonly perceived as the "sixth sense" because it controls the higher mental powers, and is related to the issues of intuition, choice, imagination, and inspiration. This center enables you to connect with the energy of the world beyond your five senses, to learn how to go beneath superficial appearances and find deeper truths, and to cultivate your inherent resources of creativity and wisdom. In these ways the sixth energy center encompasses the challenges fundamental to many Eastern spiritual traditions, as well as pagan and folk religions that rely upon divination systems—such as the I Ching, tarot, runes—to decipher the workings of intuition.

When your sixth energy center is healthy, your intuition and imagination feed into each other. More important, you are receptive to the sublime forces around you, and this fires up your creative instincts. A sixth center that is blocked or inactive manifests itself in a distrust of anything that cannot be comprehended by the rational mind. You have an obsessive need to parse out reality, the material and immaterial, into precise categories and measurements. Furthermore, you like things just the way they are; you are never inspired to imagine that the world as you know it could be different.

The brow-energy center is the place where we nurture the wisdom and spiritual purpose to make our dreams come true.

color: Indigo

location: Brow, above and between the eyes ("third eye")

developmental years: 36–42

element: Radium

sense: Intuition

physical organs: Brain, eyes, nervous system, skull

the positive (the sage): Intuitive, wise, discerning, perceptive, inspirational

the negative (the know-it-all): Judgment, know-it-all, unfeeling, ungracious

archetypes: Jonas Salk, Helen Keller, Steven Spielberg, Bill Gates, Albert Einstein, Carl Sagan, Stephen Hawking, Stevie Wonder, Ray Charles, Pablo Picasso, and scientists, surgeons, painters, philosophers, forecasters, astronomers who are involved in the intuitive or observatory or visual arts

conscious choices: Developing intuition through introspective isolation and interactive person-to-person exchange

your indigo resources

indigo aromatherapy:
Sandalwood, geranium maculatum, lavender, eucalyptus, blue chamomile

meditations and home life can be enhanced by
Indigo flowers: Irises, lilacs

indigo gemstones: Amethyst, azurite, blue and white fluorite, moonstone, purple apatite

indigo room: The quiet room

indigo exercise and moving meditations
Music should be extremely slow and orchestrated. Lie on your back on a hard surface with a pillow underneath your knees. Focus on the space between your eyes, commonly referred to as the third eye. Synchronize breathing to the music.

indigo movies and television
> *Eve's Bayou*
> *Resurrection*
> *City of Angels*
> *Apollo 13*
> *Three Wishes*
> *The House of the Spirits*

Contact
The Miracle Worker
The Secret Garden
Phenomenon
Powder
The Discovery Channel
The Sci-Fi Channel

indigo books
Anatomy of the Spirit by Caroline Myss
The Alchemist by Paulo Coelho
Mutant Message Down Under by Marlo Morgan
Sophie's World by Jostein Gaarder
Einstein's Dreams by Alan P. Lightman
Seventh Heaven by Alice Hoffman
Animal Dreams by Barbara Kingsolver
Practical Intuition by Laura Day
Awakening Intuition by Mona Lisa Schultz
Seat of the Soul by Gary Zukav

affirmations

intuition
I see better with my eyes closed.
I see solutions to all situations.
I see energy in all things.
I see intuition as my God-given gift.

imagination
I see answers to questions very clearly.
I see things others may not.
I see new ways of doing things.

decisiveness
> I see being proactive as positive and procrastination as negative.
> I see what is right for me and what is wrong for me.
> I see my decision as the right decision.

inspiration
> I see each day as an opportunity to do good things for the sake of humanity.
> I see beauty in all things and all people.
> I see life as art.

intuition

philosophy: your sixth sense wishes you
would use it more often

the positive (wise, insightful, observant, perceptive)
You are a wise soul. You enjoy spending time alone to explore your deeper thoughts, and you have a curiosity for magic and fairy tales. When you were growing up, you were exposed to the mysteries of life. You were encouraged to share your dreams and visions, no matter how bizarre. You played lots of guessing games. You were told that some things could not be learned through books because they had to be experienced. You understood that there is a difference between being smart and being wise. If you were very lucky, you even had an indigo relative or friend who introduced you to the idea of your sixth sense. You didn't think you had a guardian angel; you knew it.

the negative (know-it-all, judgmental)
You see yourself as all-knowing; no one knows more than you, including the universe. You were taught to rely upon facts

alone, and to deny the validity of feeling and instinct. According to you, the world is either black or white. Reality is only that which can be measured out into precise units. You think that believing in magic and the mystical is for idiots, because everything you need to know can be found in a book or by your five common senses. You will not acknowledge the value of your sixth sense, so it is rarely used.

conscious choices

Spend an afternoon just observing the world around you.

Start a dream journal.

Try trusting the universe by flipping a coin the next time you have a hard decision to make.

Try to mind-read—you'll be surprised at how often you will be right. My personal favorite is to write down my questions and place them under my pillow, then wait and see what my dreams tell me.

Check out a few Arthur C. Clarke books or videos.

journal questions

What does the phrase "inner voice" mean to you?

_____

_____

_____

_____

What events in your life have you sensed before they happened?

_____

_____

_____

_____

Describe a past experience where you should have listened to your inner voice.

_____

_____

_____

_____

How can you learn to hear and trust your inner voice better?

_____

_____

_____

_____

imagination

philosophy: beyond our imagination is more imagination

the positive (vision, innovation, invention)
They call you the space cowboy. You see with your eyes closed. You know that believing is seeing, and what you see is the world in a brand-new, highly unusual light. When you make your visions real, you more than likely create something new and unusual. You are known for your vivid sense of color, your unusual style, and your need to be alone to cultivate your vision.

the negative (conformity)
Not only are you not a space cowboy, but outer space does nothing for you. As a child growing up, you painted only with primary colors. If you painted a tree, it was always green instead of pink with purple polka dots. You were told never to mix checks with stripes. When it comes to putting things to-

gether, you follow instructions to the letter. You are never inspired to improve on an existing idea because you are fearful of change of any kind.

conscious choices

Write a song, even if you've never played an instrument.

Make a picture of a tree that looks like anything but a tree.

Put together an outfit you've never worn before, using colors and clothes you'd never wear.

Find a new way to drive to work.

Write a fairy tale using people, places, and things that couldn't possibly be real.

journal questions

Describe the difference between imagination and creativity.

_____

_____

_____

_____

Describe a person whom you consider to be imaginative.

_____

_____

_____

_____

Describe why you think you are an imaginative person.

_____

_____

_____

_____

_____

Describe a situation that could have turned out better if you had employed more imagination.

_____

_____

_____

_____

_____

decisiveness

philosophy: indecision is a choice

the positive (discernment, decisiveness)
You are the master of your own mind. You are perfectly comfortable making decisions. More than likely, you were pushed out into the world and trusted to make certain decisions for yourself. The message when you were growing up was that indecision *is* a decision and a cop-out that affects you negatively. Furthermore, you were told there is no such thing as a bad decision. Armed with that information, you are able to be decisive. Best of all, you are a "jump thinker" who is able to see the road ahead, so you always know which way to turn.

the negative (uncertainty, indecision, procrastination)
To be or not to be—you're still deciding. When you were growing up, all of your decisions were made for you. When the time came to decide for yourself, you were lost. "Should I or shouldn't I?" Making decisions of any kind is agonizing. Your constant fear of making the wrong decision prevents you from making any decisions at all. Over time, life has begun to stand still. You have fallen into paralyzing ruts, and procrastination has become a way of life.

conscious choices

Put a time limit on making decisions: Give yourself one
minute to make little decisions, five minutes for bigger
ones.

Be the one in a social situation to choose the things you
want—the movie, the restaurant, to be or not to be in a
relationship.

Choose to do something, anything, even if it's wrong—and
always be aware that you're the one doing the choosing.

When in doubt about a or b, choose c: the option you
hadn't considered.

journal questions

How would you describe your ability to make sound decisions?

_____

_____

_____

_____

Who is the most decisive person you know? Why?

_____

_____

_____

_____

Describe an incident in which you waited too long to make a
decision and were left with a poor choice.

_____

_____

_____

_____

_____

Make a list of all the decisions you've been putting off and how you are going to proceed.

_____

_____

_____

_____

_____

inspiration

philosophy: we inspire ourselves by inspiring others

the positive (motivation)
Your very existence is an inspiration to others. You see the world not as it is but as it should be. The belief that no matter how good things are they can always be better inspires you. You "see" that there are no limitations on anything or anybody. You believe in miracles, and you believe in yourself. You are a wild and free spirit. Your inspiration is contagious and makes others want to latch on to your world, even if they can't quite understand it.

the negative (stagnation)
No one stands in place better than you. You accept things as they are and do little, if anything, to better your circumstances. You believe that the world is the way it is and nothing can ever change it. You are content not to take chances. You cling to the known in every area of life, from career to home to personal relationships, because the easy road is far more appealing than the road that has hills and valleys and is filled with twists and turns. Playing it safe is the only way you'll play, period.

conscious choices

Take a person under your wing and help uplift him or her.

Join causes you believe in, and make a difference.

Write down your plan for the ideal world.

Read inspiring biographies, such as those about Mother Teresa, Martin Luther King, Jr., Helen Keller, and Christopher Reeve.

journal questions

What people or events have caused you to lose your inspiration?

_____

_____

_____

_____

_____

Describe inspirational people in your life or in the world.

_____

_____

_____

_____

_____

How do you inspire other people?

_____

_____

_____

_____

_____

What can you do to become a more inspiring person?

_____

_____

_____

_____

_____

breaking it down now, to avoid a breakdown later:

it's time for a change

color: indigo
issue: intuition

the choice

What is the negative choice?

The negative choice is ignoring my intuitive feelings.

Why are you making this negative choice?

I do this to avoid controversy. If I make this choice, avoid difficult decisions/situations, and conform to what I feel family, co-workers, and society expect from me, I do not have to face the consequences created by my feelings of who I am and what I need to do. I am sacrificing myself for what I believe to be the team's greater good.

What do you get out of making this negative choice?

I achieve an uneasy peace. Calm, but resentful toward those who cannot see what I see or listen fairly to what I present. Bypassing my intuition gives me the room to breathe but causes me to function at a diminished capacity. This way I do not rock the boat and people generally leave me alone.

What will you get out of breaking this negative choice?

Freedom. By breaking this habitual bad choice I will be free to create, interact, enjoy life without expending huge amounts of en-

ergy ignoring what I feel to be right. The bad part is that people will change how they behave toward me. Some people recognize only facets of one's char-acter, and if they do not meet their standards attribute less to the person as a whole.

Who or what supports you in this negative choice?

The biggest supporter of my negative choice is my living situation. I am a formerly active psychic who is living with a currently active psychic. I deliberately alter my moods and express myself differently so as not to upset the balance. When she moves out, her feelings toward me di-rectly affect whether or not I will be able to be active in our son's life. If she leaves with positive feelings, I will have full custody. If she leaves with negative feelings, I will never see him again. I am living under immense stress, in which I must deny my intuition and not take appropriate action. I feel as though I am handcuffed in every area of my life. I cannot feel free at work (where my intuition is the very fabric of what I do), dating, or even deciding what type of gasoline to put in the car. I am stifled and in a continuous state of self-denial.

How is this choice postponing the life you wish to lead?

By denying my intuition, I am limiting my progress at work, avoiding meaningful personal relationships, and not being the person I know that I am but cannot bring myself to be. It is holding back the creative maelstrom that is lurking within me. I know I can create better things, be a better parent, and support a mutually caring relationship with another adult, but my negative choice is stopping me.

the change

In order to change you must acknowledge negative behavior and forgive. For the next thirty days focus daily meditation and/or prayer on the following affirmations. Deep breathing is extremely beneficial during this time.

I am willing to release the need:
To follow others instead of myself.

I am willing to release and shed the past:
Of things I saw happen to similar people. Their experiences are not mine, and I must go forward.

I am willing to release this pattern of negativity:
And trust what is true.

I am willing to release that which is negative for me:
And take what comes from being true to myself. I will always find a way to communicate with my son, and to be myself with others.

Forgiveness and reconciliation are two different concepts. Forgiveness is a must, reconciliation is optional. When you begin your forgiveness exercises, place your hands over your heart as you recite those things you forgive. Seeing yourself and those you are forgiving as small children will help you—it's so much easier to forgive a child than an adult. (If the person you need to forgive is deceased or you're having difficulty conjuring an image of him, try focusing on a photo.)

I forgive myself for:
My self-betrayal.
Hurting others through my inaction and deliberate by-passing of my intuition.
My incredible anger.
My violent nature.
Not seeking my truth.

I forgive my mother for:

Punishing only me in our family as I expressed my individuality.

Being semi-invalid my whole life.

Teaching me to hide my gifts.

I forgive my father for:

Always traveling and not being there until I was almost in puberty.

Not giving me any direction in life (I was always told I could be whatever I wanted, but received no guidance in choosing or exploring).

Ignoring me until I was an adult.

the commitment

Never make a commitment you can't keep. Underpromise. Overdeliver. Don't seek perfection, seek a positive outcome.

the crawl

Unlocking my mind. I need to reactivate that part of me that I have locked away to avoid conflict.

the baby step

Listening. I need to begin to listen to myself again and understand that my intuitive thoughts have validity and record them appropriately.

walking

Thinking. I need to respond to intuitive thoughts by assessing how they fit the situation and the outcome of their actuation. Learn to differentiate between paranoia and intuition.

running

Starting to trust my intuition on smaller choices (broccoli or corn?). Let answers begin to flow again. See what happens.

taking flight

Facing those situations I am avoiding with faith in my abilities and myself. Being free to be myself.

affirmations

Love yourself. Believe in yourself. All is well.

There is always a choice.
Conflict is not insurmountable.
Things are better than they seem.

breaking it down now, to avoid a breakdown later:

it's time for a change

color: _____
issue: _____

the choice

What is the negative choice?

_____
_____
_____

Why are you making this negative choice?

_____
_____
_____

What do you get out of making this negative choice?

_____
_____
_____

What will you get out of breaking this negative choice?

_____
_____
_____

Who or what supports you in this negative choice?

_____

_____

_____

How does your past support this negative choice?

_____

_____

_____

How is this negative choice postponing the life you wish to lead?

_____

_____

_____

the change

In order to change you must acknowledge negative behavior and forgive. For the next thirty days focus daily meditation and/or prayer on the following affirmations. Deep breathing is extremely beneficial during this time.

I am willing to release the need to:

_____

_____

_____

_____

I am willing to release and shed the past:

_____

_____

_____

_____

I am willing to release this pattern of negativity:

_____

_____

_____

_____

I am willing to release that which is negative for me:

_____

_____

_____

_____

Forgiveness and reconciliation are two different concepts. Forgiveness is a must, reconciliation is optional. When you begin your forgiveness exercises, place your hands over your heart as you recite those things you forgive. Seeing yourself and those you are forgiving as small children will help you—it's so much easier to forgive a child than an adult. (If the person you need to forgive is deceased or you're having difficulty conjuring an image of him, try focusing on a photo.)

I forgive myself for:

_____

_____

_____

_____

I forgive my mother for:

_____

_____

_____

_____

I forgive my father for:

_____

_____

_____

_____

I forgive my _____ (other) for:

_____

_____

_____

_____

the commitment

Never make a commitment you can't keep. Underpromise.
Overdeliver. Don't seek perfection, seek a positive outcome.

the crawl

_____

_____

the baby step

_____

_____

the first step

_____

_____

walking

_____

_____

running

_____

_____

taking flight

_____

_____

affirmations

_____

_____

_____

_____

_____

violet
selflessness

philosophy: God's plans are always
better than our own.

Violet is the color of trust and surrender. Like indigo, violet is a color that is often absent from our daily visual field of color. A color often worn by the holy during religious ceremonies, violet is also given to us in a variety of different flowers. It is not a coincidence that flowers are presented as an expression of gratitude or thanks, but also during the painful times of death and surrender. And who can forget the Purple Heart, a medal of honor given to those whose actions proved them willing to sacrifice their life for their country.

Violet is the seventh color of the rainbow and is associated with our seventh and final energy center, which is located at the crown. This energy center is dominant during the years forty-three to forty-nine and beyond. The crown center is the site at which we are connected with the energy of the Divine. The energy from this center provides us with the deepest knowledge possible about our purpose in life and how it relates to the truths of the universe. The issues this center controls are surrender, gratitude, faith, and humility. The spirit of the crown center ultimately boils down to the principle of letting go and accepting the will of the Divine, which is at the heart of a wide spectrum of faiths, including Christianity, Judaism, Islam, Buddhism, Hinduism, and Native American religions. Islam, with its holiday of Ramadan, a monthlong religious observance that calls for fasting daily from dawn to sunset, and its requirement of five prayer sessions a day, offers a supreme example of the idea of personal sacrifice and surrender.

If your crown center is highly developed, you believe in the rightness of your world; you are confident that things will always work out because you have placed your trust in the Divine. Your time spent praying and meditating has been time well spent, for it has given you an insight into the oneness, or interconnectedness, of all reality. If you have not nurtured your crown center, you do not have a solid sense of purpose. Because you are unable to let go and give in to a spiritual reality that is larger than you, you find yourself in a perennial state of uncertainty and anxiety: You try to force things instead of letting them unfold; you fight instead of surrendering. Ultimately, you find yourself alienated from the world around you, because its "game plan" of acceptance, surrender, and unity seems like no plan at all to you.

The seventh energy center teaches us that we are all connected, and that there is a Divine presence who has a plan for us all.

color: Violet

location: Crown (top of the head)

developmental years: 43–49

element: Magnesium

sense: Energy or spiritual awareness

physical organs: Spinal cord, brain stem, nerves

the positive (the saints): Surrender, release, faith, gratitude

the negative (the sinners): Fighting, obsession, predicting, egotism, manipulation archetypes: Mother Teresa, Gandhi, the Dalai Lama, Pope John Paul II, yogis, monks, rabbis, priests, nuns, pastors, Zen masters, swamis, lamas

conscious choices: Prayer, meditation, sacrifice of worldly goods and services

your violet resources

violet aromatherapy: Freesia, olibanum, sweet violet, lavender, clary sage

violet foods: Eggplant, arugula, blackberries

meditations and home life can be enhanced by
violet flowers: Violets

violet gemstones: Amethyst

violet room: Any space in your home that is sacred to you

violet exercise and moving meditations
Music is soft and gentle. Gregorian chants are ideal. This is a lying meditation; it involves no movement. Once you lie down, try not to move at all. Focus on your crown area. Synchronize breathing to the music.

violet movies and television
  Miracle on 34th Street
  Sophie's Choice
  Ghost
  E.T.
  Field of Dreams

Saving Private Ryan
Forrest Gump
Gandhi
The Color Purple
The Song of Bernadette
Quality religious programming

violet books
The Color Purple by Alice Walker
Healing Words by Larry Dossey, M.D.
Joshua by Joseph F. Girzone
By the River Piedra I Sat Down and Wept by Paulo Coelho
Conversations with God by Neale Donald Walsch
Siddhartha by Hermann Hesse
The Road Less Traveled by M. Scott Peck

affirmations

surrender
I trust the will of God.
I trust that what is mine will come to me.
I trust the good intentions of those who love me.
I trust and surrender to love.

patience
I trust that everything will be okay, no matter what.
I trust other people to do what is right for them and for me.
I trust myself.
I trust all things to come at the appropriate time.

faith
I trust in faith.
I trust that all things happen for a reason.

I trust that the divine is always working through me.
I trust that there is always a gift attached to any painful event; therefore, I thank God for all events.

gratitude
I trust in the grace of God.
I trust in the graciousness of those who love me.
I trust that to live in grace is to live in peace.

surrender

philosophy: I will, thy will

the positive (release)
You're wise enough to know that the only battle is the battle within, and you choose not to fight yourself. You believe that all things happen for a reason. You are certain that when one door closes, another one will always open. You remain unattached to your worldly possessions, and you have come to terms with the inevitability of death. You view loss as gain and see crisis as opportunity.

the negative (manipulation, obsession, anxiety)
You're the master of manipulation. You can't let things just be as they are. If a door won't open, you kick it open. You lose sleep at night obsessing about the outcomes of personal and professional situations. Going with the flow is not your thing; you push against the river. When you encounter opposition, you must always get your way, often through manipulation and making others feel guilty. Not surprisingly, you are an extremely sore loser and an incessant worrywart.

conscious choices

Practice "giving in" more.

Accept defeat graciously.

Give away something you absolutely love.

Give up something you really want to do to accommodate something else.

Concede in a long-standing battle in which you are engaged.

journal questions

Describe a situation in which you would have been better off surrendering rather than fighting.

_____

_____

_____

_____

Whom do you know who practices surrender as a way of life?

_____

_____

_____

_____

Describe a situation in which you surrendered to the will of God.

_____

_____

_____

_____

What or whom do you need to surrender to at the present time?

_____

_____

_____

patience

philosophy: timing is everything

the positive (acceptance)
You are a timeless individual. It would not surprise anybody that you rarely wear a watch. You know that time is space and space is time, and the past, present, and future are one. You have been taught to take "the road less traveled." Cutting corners or being in a hurry makes no sense in your world. You wait as long as you have to for windows and doors to open, knowing they always will. You force nothing, because you view time as your ally, and you know instinctively that what is yours will eventually come to you.

the negative (anxiety)
Time is your enemy. In the realm of personal and professional relationships it is now or never, and never is usually the winner. You can't allow anything to just unfold. You open presents before holidays, eat food that is undercooked, and live in a constant state of agitation. You have an impatience to know everything, even things you aren't supposed to know. You do not use psychics, astrology, or mediums judiciously; you use them constantly.

conscious choices
    Stop wearing a watch.
    Plan hour by hour.
    Drive more slowly.

Walk at a more leisurely pace.
Make a meal last twice as long.
Take a seat in the time-out chair.

journal questions

Describe a situation or an event in which you tried to control the outcome rather than just letting things happen.

_____

_____

_____

_____

_____

Describe your impression of a person who never worries.

_____

_____

_____

_____

Describe a present situation in which you would be better served by being patient and releasing control.

_____

_____

_____

_____

_____

What can you do in order to stop obsessing and start releasing?

_____

_____

_____

_____

_____

faith

philosophy: hope is desperation; faith is relaxation

the positive (trust, openness)
You live by faith. You never hope for anything, because you place your faith in God and you know in your heart that everything will work out. You believe in only the very best for you, for the people you love, and even for the people you don't love. No matter how bad things get, you never give up on yourself or God. You believe only in good beginnings and happy endings.

the negative (distrust, snooping, scrutinizing)
You are judge and jury. You see only the worst in people and events, if you see anything at all. You trust no one. You always want the bad news first. You are certain things will turn out badly and that nothing ever goes right anyway. God, or a higher spiritual force, plays little or no role in your life because distrust and faith can't exist side by side.

conscious choices
    Go to a house of worship.
    Pray.
    Read books on the healing power of prayer.
    Practice being more trusting.
    Put time aside each day for sitting, deep meditation.

journal questions

What people or events in your life have caused you to lose faith?

_____

_____

_____

Describe people you know who live by the power of faith instead of the power of people.

_____

_____

_____

_____

Describe the quality of your faith.

_____

_____

_____

Describe how living by faith, and not hope, could enhance the quality of your life.

_____

_____

_____

_____

gratitude

philosophy: thank God

the positive (graciousness)
You live in a state of grace. No moment in your life is experienced without a sense of reverence and wonder. More than likely, you were taught to pray at an early age. There were prayers at dinner, prayers before bed, and sometimes prayers upon rising. You were thankful for everything and everybody.

You were taught to have a great reverence for all things in this world, living and nonliving. You were taught to say thank you to other people often, but thank you to God always.

the negative (ungraciousness)

You take everything for granted. Nothing is ever good enough for you. The cup is always half empty instead of half full. You are ungracious about everything, from a good breakfast to a sunny day. You rarely say thank you when it is socially appropriate, and as for thank-you notes—forget it. You pray only when absolutely necessary, and only for yourself. Your life is one long string of expectations unfulfilled.

conscious choices

Begin saying grace before each meal.

Start a gratitude journal. Make a list of all the people you take for granted in your life.

Set up a sacred space in your home.

Live each day as if it were your last.

Write thank you notes.

journal questions

Describe a situation in which you or someone else you know displayed a lack of gratitude.

_____

_____

_____

_____

Describe the most gracious person you know.

_____

_____

_____

How would people describe your graciousness?

Make a list of all the people you'd thank if you had only six months to live. Thank them!

What other things can you do to become a more grateful person?

breaking it down now, to avoid a breakdown later:

it's time for a change

color: violet
issue: faith

the choice
We choose our life.

What is the negative choice?
constant obsessing about another person's/persons' relationship with my partner. Jealousy.

Why are you making this negative choice?
I don't know why. I am not always aware of making this negative choice; something irrational drives me. It seems like an automatic response, especially noticeable when I am not feeling good about myself.

What do you get out of making this negative choice?
control. Speaking my piece about who gets to call the house. Reinforcement and attention from my partner.

What will you get out of breaking this negative choice?
Peace. A sense of unshakable worth.

Who or what supports you in this negative choice?
Partner. Enjoys the attention of this person.

How does your past support this negative choice?

Totally being hurt and betrayed in all serious love relationships. Never had a relationship with my father, therefore constantly seeking male approval and guidance.

How is this negative choice postponing the life you wish to lead?

The life I wish to lead is so full of inner joy and success, there is no time, need, or feeling to have these negative thoughts.

the change

In order to change you must acknowledge negative behavior and forgive. For the next thirty days focus daily meditation and/or prayer on the following affirmations. Deep breathing is extremely beneficial during this time.

I am willing to release the need to:

Constantly obsess about my current partner and feel jealous.

I am willing to release and shed the past:

In order to live up to my full potential I need to come to terms with some deep-rooted past issues. Until I accomplish this, I feel I cannot move forward and I will keep repeating old patterns.

I am willing to release this pattern of negativity:

There comes a time in everyone's life when one gets tired of feeling unworthy because one is not yet what one should become. The time has come to dispose of negative thoughts and patterns and to have a solid foundation of new thinking for a joyful future.

Forgiveness and reconciliation are two different concepts. Forgiveness is a must, reconciliation is optional. When you begin your forgiveness exercises, place your hands over your heart as you recite those things you forgive. Seeing yourself and those you are forgiving as small children will help you—it's so much easier to forgive a child than an adult. (If the person you need to forgive is deceased or you're having difficulty conjuring an image of him, try focusing on a photo.)

I forgive myself for:

Wasting prime time with the wrong guys desperately hoping for their approval.

Allowing others to treat me like a doormat.

Not believing in myself enough to finish college and get a professional degree.

Lying about my background and other things because of shame.

"Giving in" on issues that were important to me.

Trying to reinvent myself for other people when I could have been creatively using my time.

I forgive my mother for:

Her constant judging of men who came into my life who she decided were not good enough for me.

Her negative, intrusive opinions that caused confusion for me.

Never approving of any of my chosen mates.

Trying to control my life.

I forgive my father for:

His total neglect.

His weakness and substance abuse.

Never providing me with gifts that made me feel special.

the commitment

Never make a commitment you can't keep. Underpromise. Overdeliver. Don't seek perfection, seek a positive outcome.

the crawl
Daily affirmations. Forgiving Mother, Father, and myself every A.M. Reaffirming faith.

the baby step
Making peace with my father. Releasing the past. Asking for his forgiveness for harboring negative feelings about him.

the first step
Phone protocol for me. After a phone call for my partner, do not ask the question "Who was that?" Do not ask the question "What did they want?"

walking
Getting partner to agree to setting boundaries with female friends that are comfortable for both of us.

running
I will be running forward when I feel a greater sense of self-worth. Feeling a sense of accomplishment helps me. I am best at creative things, therefore my focus shall be on developing that talent in myself.

taking flight
Taking the next solid step to getting partner to agree on legally committing to the relationship. If he is unable to do so, I will go forward without him with the caveat that when he is ready he should contact me, and if I'm still interested I will consider his proposal.

affirmations
Love yourself. Believe in yourself. All is well.
I am proud of who I am.

No one is a threat to my relationship with my mate.
I am moving forward in my life in a healthy, positive manner.
I am a creative, intelligent, attractive, successful woman.
God guides me in all my positive thoughts and actions.
I will be given all that I need.

breaking it down now, to avoid a breakdown later:

it's time for a change

color: _____
issue: _____

the choice

What is the negative choice?

_____
_____
_____

Why are you making this negative choice?

_____
_____
_____

What do you get out of making this negative choice?

_____
_____
_____

What will you get out of breaking this negative choice?

_____
_____
_____

Who or what supports you in this negative choice?

_____

_____

_____

How is this negative choice postponing the life you wish to lead?

_____

_____

_____

the change

In order to change you must acknowledge negative behavior and forgive. For the next thirty days focus daily meditation and/or prayer on the following affirmations. Deep breathing is extremely beneficial during this time.

I am willing to release the need to:

_____

_____

_____

_____

I am willing to release and shed the past:

_____

_____

_____

_____

I am willing to release this pattern of negativity:

_____

_____

I am willing to release that which is negative for me:

_____

_____

_____

_____

_____

Forgiveness and reconciliation are two different concepts. Forgiveness is a must, reconciliation is optional. When you begin your forgiveness exercises, place your hands over your heart as you recite those things you forgive. Seeing yourself and those you are forgiving as small children will help you—it's so much easier to forgive a child than an adult. (If the person you need to forgive is deceased or you're having difficulty conjuring an image of him, try focusing on a photo.)

I forgive myself for:

_____

_____

_____

I forgive my mother for:

_____

_____

_____

I forgive my father for:

_____

_____

_____

I forgive my _____ (other) for:

_____

_____

_____

the commitment
Never make a commitment you can't keep. Underpromise. Overdeliver. Don't seek perfection, seek a positive outcome.

the crawl

_____

_____

the baby step

_____

_____

the first step

_____

_____

walking

_____

_____

running

_____

_____

taking flight

_____

_____

affirmations

_____
_____
_____
_____
_____

part iii

---

m a i n t e n a n c e

the rainbow:
the eighth wonder
of the world

philosophy: let there be light.

When you combine the seven colors of the rainbow, you end up with the eighth wonder of the world: pure light.

The nature of true enlightenment is exemplified by individuals who are seen as true rainbow beings. They are light in spirit, bringing little to no baggage.

They are red with honor and respect.
They are orange with a sense of well-being and happiness.
They are yellow with a strong sense of leadership and confidence.
They are green with compassion and generosity.
They are blue with integrity and curiosity.
They are indigo with a strong sense of vision and information.
They are violet with a deep sense of gratitude and faith.

But the one quality they exude that holds together all the other qualities is their undeniable sense of humility.

Humility allows others to feel connected to your light, and humility, above all else, allows us to feel connected to God's light.

the road ahead:
self-discipline

philosophy: your journey is not over, until it's over.

Y ou've completed the first leg of your journey. However, rainbows can disappear just as quickly as they appear. For this reason, holding on to your rainbow will require the commitment of constant attention. You will find the affirmation cards to be an invaluable tool in making your rainbow a permanent part of your life.

You can use the twenty-eight cards for maintenance in the following ways:

daily
Choose a card every day and try to bring that particular color and the issue(s) into your life for that day. Refer to the beginning of each chapter for color resources.

weekly
Select one of the twenty-eight affirmation cards and focus on that particular color issue for the week. Make a list of the proactive choices you wish to accomplish for that week.

monthly
For the person who has completed the twenty-eight-day program but genuinely feels that a particular energy center is blocked, a monthly program is recommended. Refer back to the chart "The Anatomy of Your Rainbow," which will help you figure out if there is a blocked energy center. Once you have established the particular dysfunctional center(s), you will

choose one center per month to stay focused on, utilizing your work sheets.

the road ahead: self-preservation

It is very difficult to address people in your life who are behaving in a way that is negative for you. It's also difficult to remember that your goal should not be to try to change them. Rather, your goal needs to be to change the situation by addressing *your needs* and then creating boundaries. Frequently it is easier not to do this verbally. If that is the case, write a letter. It's easier and you can practice as many times as necessary. The important thing to remember is to make your letter loving (green). People behaving negatively are in more trouble than you. Often the kindest thing you can do is to wish them well while removing yourself from their negativity. As always, remember these suggestions are best incorporated into a plan that has been formulated with professional help.

The following are examples of language you can use in letters:

emotional/physical abuse

"Having you in my life does not give you permission to treat me badly. I need to be happy and feel safe, and unless you can change your behavior I cannot see or speak with you."

addiction

"Having you in my life is causing me great sadness, aggravation, and is making me feel like a failure. I cannot allow myself to feel this way. I need to feel positive every day of my life. I will not allow one more second of your negative behavior to be a part of my life. I hope you can get things straightened out, but until such time I will not see you or speak to you again. In order to have a relationship with me you can never, and I mean

never, drink/drug/not work/be abusive/lie/cheat again. I wish
you well."

forgiveness

"Having you in my life did not give you permission to betray
my trust. I'm sorry you were not strong enough to be truthful;
however, I hope we can both learn from this difficult lesson and
that we are both able to heal. I forgive you and I forgive myself, but we do not need to repeat this mistake again. I'm moving on. I feel no anger, but in the interest of self-preservation I
am unable to speak to you at the present time. I wish you
well."

asking for forgiveness

"I humbly ask for your forgiveness. My behavior was greatly
flawed and it has now caused you, a person I value, great harm.
I have a lot of work to do. I must face the mirror, for better or
worse, and come to terms with myself for failing you. Until I
can be certain that I will not hurt you again, I must remain estranged from you. Even if I am able to pull myself together, I
will understand if your feelings of self-preservation lead you to
choose not to have me in your life. I wish you the very best."

summary

By the time I finished writing this book, two miracles oc-
curred. The first miracle is that I became a first-time home-
owner. The home I purchased was bought sight unseen. A
strange way to buy a first home, but I trust God implicitly. I
knew when I got the call from my mom that it was really God
who was calling. God delivered me a small, quaint home that
felt divine in every way. On the day I took possession, all of the
flowers had died due to the hot Arizona sun. Nevertheless, in

the backyard a strange patch of bright violet flowers remained. A color cue for me, considering the gratitude I felt for being guided to such an exquisite home. More important, I knew that my violet issues were in front of me and would require my commitment. The second miracle is seeing the daily rainbow prisms that dance off my garage door. My House of Color is a real house once again.

If there has been a secret to my own personal happiness, it has been this: My expectations have never been grand. I am totally taken with the violet flowers in my backyard and the hummingbird that now greets me each morning. For me, these are the big things in life. In the same way, I try to celebrate the ordinary person who takes even baby steps to be good. I view mistakes as good and success as a benediction. As for regrets, I don't believe in looking back. It's over.

As for the miracles you were promised at the beginning of the book, there is no better way to make them happen than living by the sentiments expressed in one of my favorite books: *By the River Piedra I Sat Down and Wept:*

> You have to take risks, he said. We will only understand the miracle of life fully when we allow the unexpected to happen.
>
> Every day, God gives us the sun—and also one moment in which we have the ability to change everything that makes us unhappy. Every day, we try to pretend that we haven't perceived that moment, that it doesn't exist—that today is the same as yesterday and will be the same as tomorrow. But if people really pay attention to their everyday lives, they will discover that magic moment. It may arrive in the instant when we are doing something mundane, like putting our front-door key in the lock; it may lie hidden in the quiet that follows the lunch hour or in the thousand and one

things that all seem the same to us. But that moment exists—a moment when all the power of the stars becomes a part of us and enables us to perform miracles.

Joy is sometimes a blessing, but it is often a conquest. Our magic moment helps us to change and sends us off in search of our dreams. Yes, we are going to suffer, we will have difficult times, and we will experience many disappointments—but all of this is transitory; it leaves no p ermanent mark. And one day we will look back with pride and faith at the journey we have taken.

Pitiful is the person who is afraid of taking risks. Perhaps this person will never be disappointed or disillusioned; perhaps she won't suffer the way people do when they have a dream to follow. But when that person looks back—and at some point everyone looks back—she will hear her heart saying, "What have you done with the miracles that God planted in your days? What have you done with the talents God bestowed on you? You buried yourself in a cave because you were fearful of losing those talents. So this is your heritage: the certainty that you wasted your life."

Pitiful are the people who must realize this. Because when they are finally able to believe in miracles, their life's magic moments will have already passed them by.

It is my hope that you now know in your heart that you are an MIP—a miracle in progress, and that you are now ready to make the conscious choices that will manifest your miracles every day.

support yourself

appendices

chakra basics:
energy = chi = prana

The idea of a fundamental energy force flowing through us has been a mainstay of Eastern thought for millennia. The Indians describe this absolute energy as prana, while the Chinese and Japanese refer to the universal life energy force Chi, or Ki, that is the source of all energy and whose flows are responsible for who we are. Homeopathy refers to it as the vital force.

While the idea of an absolute energy force is central to many spiritual traditions, it is perhaps the ancient Indian system of the seven energy centers which offers the most accessible and immediately practical approach to understanding this force and the way it works in humans. According to ancient Indian teachings, these seven energy centers, or chakras (which means "wheels of light" in Sanskrit), govern the generation and processing of energy in order to maintain our physical, emotional, and spiritual systems. They are located in the spine—from its base through the crown of the head—and are responsible for who and what we are, how we look at things, what we like, why we act the way we do. Like the rainbow, the energy centers are considered the point where the energy of the heavens and the earth meet. They ensure that we are in constant exchange with the energy systems of our environment. In a sense, they are a vast network of information processors. In my mind, this is the real "information highway." It is far more sophisticated than any computer we know.

Additionally, everyone has an energy field, or aura, that surrounds their body. It is composed of four interpenetrating layers: the etheric—the site of the seven energy centers, the emotional, the mental, and the spiritual. The energy centers take energy from the subtle bodies, the environment, and the cosmos and convert it into the frequencies needed to sustain the body's physical and psychic health. In this way, the human body is the center of a continual interaction between his own energies and those of the world around him.

Ideally, your energy centers are aligned properly and energy flows unimpeded throughout them—when there is no blockage, physical and spiritual health result. But when particular emotional issues such as fear, jealousy, and anger block the free flow of energy, health problems arise. As the medical intuitive Caroline Myss has astutely observed, "Our biography is our biology."

Let's look at the emotional and physical coordinates of the seven centers and the diseases that are most often associated with them:

red

Red corresponds to the root center, which is located at the base of the spine, between the anus and the genitals. This is the center that controls our foundations, emotional and physical, where issues of security and stability originate. Its terrain is the spinal column, rectum, legs, bones, feet, and immune system, all of which are imperative in defending the body from harm.

orange

Orange corresponds to the sacral center, located in the region between the lower abdomen and the navel area. Orange is the center that controls issues of self-control and personal well-being. As Caroline Myss points out, the illnesses that originate in this energy center are "activated by the fear of losing control. Prostate or ovarian cancer, chronic pain in the lower back and hips, and arthritis . . . problems at menopause, such as hot flashes and depression" are some of the prominent second center dysfunctions.

yellow

Yellow corresponds to the solar plexus center and is located in the area that encompasses the stomach, pancreas, liver, gallbladder, upper intestines, spleen, and abdomen. The illnesses that originate in this area are rooted in the inability to establish personal boundaries and a sense of self-worth. Thus, diseases of the liver and the digestive system are the most common solar plexus center physical afflictions. This is not surprising, as these are physiological mechanisms that help us sort out the food that we ingest, separating the good from the bad; when our sense of personal power has been disrupted, we are vulnerable to the machinations of others and lose the ability to sort out what is right for us and what is wrong for us.

green

Green corresponds to the heart center and is located at the center of the chest. This area encompasses the heart, breasts, ribs, lungs, diaphragm, thymus, and circulatory system. The heart center revolves around issues of self-love and empathy; when it is functioning harmoniously, it gives us the strength to let go of grievances and resentments and let love and compassion flow through us. Accordingly, the physical ailments that originate here tend to involve problems with circulation and openness: heart attacks, heart disease, and even cancer, a disease that some link to issues such as bitterness, anger, and resentment—the opposite of positive heart center energy.

blue

Blue corresponds to the throat center and is located at the throat. This area encompasses the throat, thyroid, jaw, trachea, bronchial tubes, upper lungs, and esophagus. This center governs individual expression in its creative and lawful modes; accordingly, the throat is the locus of ailments that characterize this center. It is no coincidence that all of our most addictive habits also pass through this region: smoking, drugs, overeating, alcoholism, for in their own way, these ailments signify the distortions of the power of the will—the flipside of positive self-expression.

indigo

Indigo corresponds to the brow center—also known as the site of the third eye—and is located in the center of the forehead. This is the terrain of the brain, the central nervous system, the pituitary and pineal glands, and the eyes, ears, and nose. Since the brow center controls issues of intuition, intelligence, and imagination, its manifestation on the physical plane is not as apparent as with the previous centers. Oftentimes, illnesses that originate in this center involve nervous system disorders and psychological distortions. One very real consequence of misdirected energies in this center is a loss of touch with reality: You are so wrapped up in the realm of your own intellect that you are unable to comprehend a more holistic view of the real world, one that encompasses others' emotions, spiritual reflections, and subtler levels of perception. It is not uncommon for such psychic isolation to lead to a state of psychosis, or at least, severe neurosis.

violet

Violet corresponds to the crown center, which is located at the center of the top of the head. According to the Hindus, this region is the portal through which the life force enters the body. This energy impacts the entire body, on both physical and psychic levels; it affects the nervous system, the muscular system, skin, and the skeletal structure. While there are no specific illnesses that are linked to the crown center, it cannot be denied that a direct correlation exists between a blockage in this center—manifested in feelings of fear, purposelessness, or anxiety—and the body's ability to function. It is the possibility of faith in a power that is bigger than us, of gratitude for the mere fact of being alive, of letting go of our egos and opening up to divine energy that gives us the will to continue and sustains the body in that mission. It's as simple as that.

the color combinations

Now that you've learned to see your lives in terms of the seven colors of the rainbow, some of you may ask, "What about the numerous permutations within the spectrum of the primary colors? What about fuchsia, or puce, or cobalt? What are the qualities inherent in these combinations?"

Here are seven combinations of colors for those of you who feel that your predominant traits fall between these colors. If you are someone who is strongly secure as well as focused on your well-being, you will most likely be a shade of puce, the combination of red and orange. Furthermore, the combination of the characteristics of the two colors gives you a phenomenal sense of personal security.

While a complete breakdown of every possible color combination is beyond the scope of this book, the following list will give you an idea of how to interpret the presence of multiple color patterns in your life.

the color combinations

red + orange = puce = phenomenally secure

orange + yellow = peach = phenomenally entertaining

yellow + green = chartreuse = phenomenally empowered

green + blue = aqua = phenomenally motivating

blue + indigo = cobalt = phenomenally creative

indigo + violet = purple = phenomenally healing

violet + red = fuchsia = phenomenally charismatic

the major break

---

the color: all colors
my issues:

red: _____
orange: _____
yellow: _____
green: _____
blue: _____
indigo: _____
violet: _____

the choice

What is the negative choice?

_____

_____

_____

Why are you making this negative choice?

_____

_____

_____

What do you get out of making this negative choice?

_____

_____

_____

What will you get out of breaking this negative choice?

_____

_____

_____

Who or what supports you in this negative choice?

_____

_____

_____

How does your past support this negative choice?

_____

_____

_____

How is this negative choice postponing the life you wish to lead?

_____

_____

_____

the change

In order to change you must acknowledge negative behavior and forgive. For the next thirty days focus daily meditation and/or prayer on the following affirmations. Deep breathing is extremely beneficial during this time.

I am willing to release the need to:

_____

_____

_____

_____

I am willing to release and shed the past:

_____

_____

_____

_____

I am willing to release this pattern of negativity and avoidance of hard reality:

_____

_____

_____

_____

_____

Forgiveness and reconciliation are two different concepts. Forgiveness is a must, reconciliation is optional. When you begin your forgiveness exercises, place your hands over your heart as you recite those things you forgive. Seeing yourself and those you are forgiving as small children will help you—it is so much easier to forgive a child than an adult. (If the person you need to forgive is deceased or you're having difficulty conjuring an image of him, try focusing on a photo.)

I forgive myself for:

_____

_____

_____

I forgive my mother for:

_____

_____

_____

I forgive my father for:

_____

_____

_____

the commitment

Never make a commitment you can't keep. Underpromise. Overdeliver. Don't seek perfection, seek a positive outcome.

the crawl

_____

_____

the baby step

_____

_____

the first step

_____

_____

walking

_____

_____

running

_____

_____

taking flight

_____

_____

affirmations

Love yourself. Believe in yourself. All is well.

_____

_____

the major break

the color: all colors
my issues:

red: _____
orange: _____
yellow: _____
green: _____
blue: _____
indigo: _____
violet: _____

the choice

What is the negative choice?

_____

_____

Why are you making this negative choice?

_____

_____

What do you get out of making this negative choice?

_____

_____

What will you get out of breaking this negative choice?

_____

_____

_____

Who or what supports you in this negative choice?

_____

_____

_____

How does your past support this negative choice?

_____

_____

_____

How is this negative choice postponing the life you wish to lead?

_____

_____

_____

the change

In order to change you must acknowledge negative behavior and forgive. For the next thirty days focus daily meditation and/or prayer on the following affirmations. Deep breathing is extremely beneficial during this time.

I am willing to release the need to:

_____

_____

_____

_____

_____

I am willing to release and shed the past:

_____

_____

_____

_____

I am willing to release this pattern of negativity and avoidance of hard reality:

_____

_____

_____

_____

Forgiveness and reconciliation are two different concepts. Forgiveness is a must, reconciliation is optional. When you begin your forgiveness exercises, place your hands over your heart as you recite those things you forgive. Seeing yourself and those you are forgiving as small children will help you—it is so much easier to forgive a child than an adult. (If the person you need to forgive is deceased or you're having difficulty conjuring an image of him, try focusing on a photo.)

I forgive myself for:

_____

_____

_____

I forgive my mother for:

_____

_____

_____

I forgive my father for:

_____

_____

_____

the commitment
Never make a commitment you can't keep. Underpromise. Overdeliver. Don't seek perfection, seek a positive outcome.

the crawl

_____

_____

the baby step

_____

_____

the first step

_____

_____

walking

_____

_____

running

_____

_____

taking flight

_____

_____

affirmations
Love yourself. Believe in yourself. All is well.

_____

_____

_____

_____

_____

the major break
the color: all colors
my issues:

red: _____

orange: _____

yellow: _____

green: _____

blue: _____

indigo: _____

violet: _____

the choice

What is the negative choice?

_____

_____

_____

Why are you making this negative choice?

_____

_____

_____

What do you get out of making this negative choice?

_____

_____

_____

What will you get out of breaking this negative choice?

_____

_____

_____

Who or what supports you in this negative choice?

_____

_____

_____

How does your past support this negative choice?

_____

_____

_____

How is this negative choice postponing the life you wish to lead?

_____

_____

_____

the change

In order to change you must acknowledge negative behavior and forgive. For the next thirty days focus daily meditation and/or prayer on the following affirmations. Deep breathing is extremely beneficial during this time.

I am willing to release the need to:

_____

_____

_____

_____

_____

I am willing to release and shed the past:

_____

_____

_____

_____

I am willing to release this pattern of negativity and avoidance of hard reality:

_____

_____

_____

_____

Forgiveness and reconciliation are two different concepts. Forgiveness is a must, reconciliation is optional. When you begin your forgiveness exercises, place your hands over your heart as you recite those things you forgive. Seeing yourself and those you are forgiving as small children will help you—it is so much easier to forgive a child than an adult. (If the person you need to forgive is deceased or you're having difficulty conjuring an image of him, try focusing on a photo.)

I forgive myself for:

_____

_____

_____

I forgive my mother for:

_____

_____

_____

I forgive my father for:

_____

_____

_____

the commitment

Never make a commitment you can't keep. Under promise. Overdeliver. Don't seek perfection, seek a positive outcome.

the crawl

_____

_____

the baby step

_____

_____

the first step

_____

_____

walking

_____

_____

running

_____

_____

taking flight

_____

_____

affirmations
Love yourself. Believe in yourself. All is well.

_____

_____

_____

_____

recommended reading

The Bible
The Koran
The Torah
The Tao te Ching
The Sutras
The Bhagavad-Gita
The Vedas
The Upanishads

recommended programs

Native American Healings by Gwen Moon
P.O. Box 610, LaVerkin, UT 84754
(435) 635-7810

Barbara Brenner School of Healing
P.O. Box 2005, East Hampton, NY 11937
(516) 329-0951

Classes, Workshops, and Private Consultations in Energy Healing by Thomas Claire
Claire Fontaine Inc., P.O. Box 1040, Grand Central Station, New York, NY 10163-1040
(212) 647-9757

The Heart Awakening by Raoult Bertrand
P.O. Box 2005, Cave Creek, AZ 85331
(800) 370-5479

recommended therapist-referral information

American Psychiatric Association/(202) 682-6800
American Psychological Association/(202) 336-5700
National Association of Social Workers/(800) 638-8799
American Association for Marriage and Family Therapy/(202) 452-0109

organizations for further help

American Self-Help Clearinghouse
St. Clare's-Riverside Medical Center
Denville, NJ 07834
(201) 625-7101

National Self-Help Clearinghouse
25 West 43rd St., Room 620
New York, NY 10036
(212) 642-2944

aids

AIDS Hotline
(800) 342-2437

Children with AIDS
Project of America
4020 N. 20th St., Ste. 101
Phoenix, AZ 85016
(602) 265-4859
Hotline: (602) 843-8654

The Names Project—AIDS Quilt
(800) 872-6263

National AIDS Network
(800) 342-2437

Project Inform
19655 Market St., Ste. 220
San Francisco, CA 94103
(415) 558-8669

PWA Coalition
50 W. 17th St.
New York, NY 10011
(800) 828-3280

Spanish AIDS Hotline
(800) 344-7432

TDD (Hearing-Impaired)
AIDS Hotline
(800) 243-7889

alcohol abuse

Al-Anon Family Headquarters
200 Park Ave. South
New York, NY 10003
(804) 563-1600

Alcoholics Anonymous (AA)
General Service Office
475 Riverside Dr.
New York, NY 10115
(212) 870-3400

Children of Alcoholics Foundation
P.O. Box 4185, Grand Central Station
New York, NY 10163-4185
(212) 754-0656
(800) 359-COAF

Meridian Council, Inc.
Administrative Offices
4 Elmcrest Terrace
Norwalk, CT 06850

National Association of Children of Alcoholics (NACOA)
11426 Rockville Pike, Ste. 100
Rockville, MD 20852
(301) 468-0985

National Clearinghouse for Alcohol and
Drug Information (NCADI)
P.O. Box 234
Rockville, MD 20852
(301) 468-2600

National Council on Alcoholism and Drug Dependency
(NCADD)
12 West 21st St.
New York, NY 10010
(212) 206-6770

anorexia/bulimia

American Anorexia/Bulimia Association, Inc.
293 Central Park West, Ste. 1R
New York, NY 10024
(212) 501-8351

National Eating Disorders Organization
6655 South Yale Avenue
Tulsa, OK 74136
(918) 481-4044

Overeaters Anonymous
National Office
6075 Zenith Ct.
Rio Rancho, NM 87124
(505) 891-2664

cancer

National Cancer Institute
(800) 4-CANCER

children's issues

Adults Molested As Children United
(AMACU)
232 East Gish Rd.
San Jose, CA 95112
(800) 422-4453

National Committee for Prevention of Child Abuse
332 South Michigan Ave., Ste. 1600
Chicago, IL 60604

Children's and Teens' Crisis Intervention
Boys' Town Crisis Hotline
(800) 448-3000

Covenant House Hotline
(800) 999-9999

Kid Save
(800) 543-7283

National Runaway and Suicide Hotline
(800) 621-4000

missing children

Missing Children—Help Center
410 Ware Blvd., Ste. 400
Tampa, FL 33619
(800) USA-KIDS

National Center for Missing and Exploited Children
1835 K St. N.W.
Washington, DC 20006
(800) 843-5678

Children with Serious Illnesses
(fulfilling wishes)

Brass Ring Society
(918) 743-3232

Make-a-Wish Foundation
(800) 332-9474

codependency

Co-Dependents Anonymous
60 E. Richards Way
Sparks, NV 89431
(602) 277-7991

death/grieving/suicide

Grief Recovery Helpline
(800) 445-4808

Grief Recovery Institute
8306 Wilshire Blvd., Ste. 21A
Beverly Hills, CA 90211
(213) 650-1234

Mothers Against Drunk Driving
(MADD)
(817) 690-6233

National Hospice Organization (NHO)
1901 Moore St., #901
Arlington, VA 22209
(703) 243-5900

National Sudden Infant Death Syndrome
Two Metro Plaza, Ste. 205
Landover, MD 20785
(800) 221-SIDS

Seasons: Suicide Bereavement
4777 Naniola Dr.
Salt Lake City, UT 84117
(801) 537-1234

debts

Debtors Anonymous
General Service Office
P.O. Box 400, Grand Central Station
New York, NY 10163-0400
(212) 642-8220

diabetes

American Diabetes Association
(800) 232-3472

drug abuse

Cocaine Anonymous
(800) 347-8998

National Cocaine-Abuse Hotline
(800) 262-2463
(800) COCAINE

National Institute of Drug Abuse (NIDA)
5600 Fishers Lane, Room 10A-39
Rockville, MD 20852
(301) 443-6245 (for information)
(800) 662-4357 (for help)

World Service Office (CA)
3740 Overland Ave., Suite C
Los Angeles, CA 90034-6337
(310) 559-5833

gambling

Gamblers Anonymous
National Council on Compulsive Gambling
444 West 59th St., Room 1521
New York, NY 10019
(212) 903-4400

health issues

Alzheimer's Disease Information
(800) 621-0379

American Chronic Pain Association
P.O. Box 850
Rocklin, CA 95677
(916) 632-0922

American Foundation of Traditional Chinese Medicine
1280 Columbus Ave., Ste. 302
San Francisco, CA 94133
(415) 776-0502

American Holistic Health Association
P.O. Box 17400
Anaheim, CA 92817
(714) 779-6152

Chopra Center for Well-Being
Deepak Chopra, M.D.
7630 Fay Ave.
La Jolla, CA 92037
(619) 551-7788

The Fetzer Institute
9292 West KL Ave.
Kalamazoo, MI 49009
(616) 375-2000

Hippocrates Health Institute
1443 Palmdale Court
West Palm Beach, FL 33411
(407) 471-8876

Hospicelink
(800) 331-1620

Institute for Noetic Sciences
P.O. Box 909, Dept. M
Sausalito, CA 94966-0909
(800) 383-1394

The Mind-Body Medical Institute
185 Pilgrim Rd.
Boston, MA 02215
(617) 632-9525

National Health Information Center
P.O. Box 1133
Washington, DC 20013-1133
(800) 336-4797

Optimum Health Care Institute
6970 Central Ave.
Lemon Grove, CA 91945
(619) 464-3346

Preventive Medicine Research Institute
Dean Ornish, M.D.
900 Bridgeway, Ste. 2
Sausalito, CA 94965
(415) 332-2525

World Research Foundation
20501 Ventura Blvd., Ste. 100
Woodland Hills, CA 91364
(818) 332-2525

impotence

Impotency Institute of America
P.O. Box 410
Bowie, MD 20718-0410
(800) 669-1603

incest

Incest Survivors Resource Network International, Inc.
P.O. Box 7375
Las Cruces, NM 88006-7375
(505) 521-4260

course in miracles counselors

Miracle Distribution Center
1141 East Ash Ave.
Fullerton, CA 92631
(714) 738-8380
(800) 359-2246

pet bereavement

Bide-A-Wee Foundation
410 E 38th St.
New York, NY
(212) 532-6395

The Animal Medical Center
510 E. 62nd St.
New York, NY 10021
(212) 838-8100

Holistic Animal Consulting Center
29 Lyman Ave.
Staten Island, NY 10305
(718) 720-5548

rape

Austin Rape Crisis Center
1824 East Oltorf
Austin, TX 78741
(512) 440-7273

sex addictions

National Council on Sexual Addictions
P.O. Box 652
Azle, TX 76098-0652
(800) 321-2066

smoking abuse

Nicotine Anonymous
2118 Greenwich St.
San Francisco, CA 94123
(415) 750-0328

spousal abuse

National Coalition Against Domestic Violence
P.O. Box 34103
Washington, DC 20043-4103
(202) 638-6388

National Domestic Violence Hotline
(800) 799-SAFE

stress reduction

The Biofeedback & Psychophysiology Clinic
The Menninger Clinic
P.O. Box 829
Topeka, KS 66601-0829
(913) 350-5000

New York Open Center
83 Spring St.
New York, NY 10012
(212) 219-2527

Omega Institute
260 Lake Dr.
Rhinebeck, NY 12572-3212
(914) 266-4444 (for information)
(800) 944-1001 (to enroll)

Rise Institute
P.O. Box 2733
Petaluma, CA 94973
(707) 765-2758

The Stress Reduction Clinic
Jon Kabat-Zinn, Ph.D.
U. Mass. Medical Center
55 Lake Ave. North
Worcester, MA 01655
(508) 856-1616
(508) 856-2656

bibliography

Bruyere, Rosalyn L. *Wheels of Light: Chakras, Auras, and the Healing Energy of the Body.* Arcadia, Calif.: Bon Productions, 1989.

Myss, Caroline. *Anatomy of the Spirit: The Seven Stages of Power and Healing.* New York: Harmony Books, 1996.

Sharamon, Shalila, and Bodo F. Baginski. *The Chakra Handbook: From Basic Understanding to Practical Application.* Wilmot, Wis.: Lotus Light Publications, 1991.

Wauters, Ambika. *Ambika's Guide to Healing and Wholeness: The Energetic Path to the Chakras and Colour.* London: Judy Piatkus Publishers, 1993.

Whelan, Richard. *The Book of Rainbows: Art, Literature, Science and Mythology.* Cobb, Calif.: First Glance Books, 1997.

White, Ruth. *Working with Your Chakras: A Physical, Emotional, and Spiritual Approach.* York Beach, Maine: Samuel Weiser, Inc., 1993.

Willis, Pauline, and Theo Gimbel. *16 Steps to Health and Energy: A Program of Color and Visual Meditation, Movement and Chakra Balance.* St. Paul, Minn.: Llewellyn Publications, 1992.

For more information on philosophy, write:
4602 E. Hammond Lane
Phoenix, AZ 85034
(800) LOVE-151
Web site: *http://www.philosophy.com*

about the author

Cristina Carlino is the visionary behind BioMedic, a leading medical skin-care company, and philosophy, the trendsetting personal wellness company. Cristina co-owns and operates both companies with her brother-in-law, David J. Watson. Cristina is currently working on the blueprints for The Art of Grace, a not-for-profit entity that helps people in need.

the rainbow
connection_{tm}

the rainbow
connection_{tm}

the rainbow
connection_{tm}

the rainbow
connection_{tm}

color: **red**
issue: **ethics**

affirmations

i have respect for all
living things.

i have a code of honor.

i have integrity.

color: **red**
issue: **family**

affirmations

i have healthy human
relationships.

i have roots.

i have the support i need.

i have a sense of community.

i have stability.

color: **red**
issue: **balance**

affirmations

i have two feet firmly
on the ground.

i have balanced energy.

i have a connection to my
male and female sides.

i have a feeling of belonging.

color: **red**
issue: **security**

affirmations

i have abundance.

i have safety.

i have nourishment
and shelter.

i have concern for
others' safety.

i have a connection to all
living things.

the rainbow
connection_{tm}

the rainbow
connection_{tm}

the rainbow
connection_{tm}

the rainbow
connection_{tm}

color: **orange**
issue: **pleasure**

affirmations

i feel pleasure when i
pamper myself.

i feel pleasure during
lovemaking.

i feel pleasure when i am
touched.

i feel pleasure when i relax.

color: **orange**
issue: **joy**

affirmations

i feel joy when i am able to
let go of every detail.

i feel joy when i laugh.

i feel joy when i dance
and sing.

i feel joy when i just
let things be.

color: **orange**
issue: **self-control**

affirmations

i feel good when i
remain flexible.

i feel good when i move
my body.

i feel good when i allow
others to control themselves.

i feel good when i am in
control of my own life.

color: **orange**
issue: **sense of
well-being**

affirmations

i feel a sense of well-being
when i take good care of myself.

i feel a sense of well-being
when i exercise and eat
healthy foods.

i feel a sense of well-being
when i look good and
feel good.

the rainbow
connection~tm~

the rainbow
connection~tm~

the rainbow
connection~tm~

the rainbow
connection~tm~

color: **yellow**

issue: **empowerment**

affirmations

i know i am worth all of the
love and kindness the
world has to offer.

i know that my presence here
on earth is of great importance.

i know better than to let
people treat me poorly.

i know what my boundaries
are and i make sure people
respect them.

color: **yellow**

issue: **self-esteem**

affirmations

i know i am the best i can be.

i know i am well liked.

i know i am a beautiful person.

i know i can do anything i
put my mind to.

color: **yellow**

issue: **information**

affirmations

i know i am capable.

i know that knowledge is power.

i know i know the answer to
the question.

i know and understand the
world around me.

color: **yellow**

issue: **achievement**

affirmations

i know i can achieve
great things.

i know that my work is a
labor of love.

i know that i take pride in
all that i do.

the rainbow
connection_{tm}

the rainbow
connection_{tm}

the rainbow
connection_{tm}

the rainbow
connection_{tm}

color: **green**
issue: **peace**

affirmations

i love the peace i feel when
communing with nature.

i love the peace and sanctity
of my home.

i love the peace i feel when
i detach myself from
material things.

i love the peace i feel when i
stop controlling others.

color: **green**
issue: **forgiveness**

affirmations

i love myself enough to
forgive myself.

i love myself enough to
forgive others.

i love the release forgiveness
gives me.

i love being accepting
of others.

color: **green**
issue: **compassion**

affirmations

i love who i am.

i love unconditionally.

i love helping others.

i love love.

color: **green**
issue: **generosity**

affirmations

i love giving to others.

i love being given to.

i love being generous in my
everyday emotions, thoughts,
and actions.

the rainbow
connection~tm~

the rainbow
connection~tm~

the rainbow
connection~tm~

the rainbow
connection~tm~

color: **blue**
issue: **sincerity**

affirmations

i express sincerity in all that
i say and do.

i express sincerity toward others.

i express sincerity regardless
of the situation.

i express sincerity because
truth is my guiding light.

color: **blue**
issue: **willpower**

affirmations

i express willpower in
all relationships.

i express willpower in
defeating bad habits.

i express willpower in order to
maintain my clarity.

i express willpower in order
to set my intentions
in motion.

color: **blue**
issue: **creativity**

affirmations

i express my creativity in
everyday life.

i express my creativity by
writing down my ideas.

i express my creativity by doing
things with my hands.

i express my creativity in
charity and love.

color: **blue**
issue: **communication**

affirmations

i express myself verbally.

i express myself through the
written word.

i express my opinions even if
they are unpopular.

i express myself without fear.

the rainbow
connection~tm~

the rainbow
connection~tm~

the rainbow
connection~tm~

the rainbow
connection~tm~

color: **indigo**
issue: **intuition**

affirmations

i see better with
my eyes closed.

i see solutions to
all situations.

i see energy in all things.

i see intuition as my
God-given gift.

color: **indigo**
issue: **imagination**

affirmations

i see answers to questions
very clearly.

i see things others may not.

i see new ways of
doing things.

color: **indigo**
issue: **decisiveness**

affirmations

i see being proactive as
the best choice.

i see what is right for me.

i see my decision as the
right decision.

color: **indigo**
issue: **inspiration**

affirmations

i see each day as an
opportunity to do good things
for the sake of humanity.

i see beauty in all things
and all people.

i see life as art.

the rainbow
connection_{tm}

the rainbow
connection_{tm}

the rainbow
connection_{tm}

the rainbow
connection_{tm}

color: **violet**
issue: **surrender**

affirmations

i trust the will of God.

i trust that what is mine will
come to me.

i trust the good intentions
of those who love me.

i trust and surrender to love.

color: **violet**
issue: **patience**

affirmations

i trust myself.

i trust that everything will be
okay, no matter what.

i trust other people to do what
is right for them and for me.

i trust all things to come at
the appropriate time.

color: **violet**
issue: **faith**

affirmations

i trust in faith.

i trust that all things
happen for a reason.

i trust that the divine is
always working through me.

i trust that there is always a
gift attached to any painful
event; therefore, i thank God
for all events.

color: **violet**
issue: **gratitude**

affirmations

i trust in the grace of God.

i trust in the graciousness of
those who love me.

i trust that to live in grace
is to live in peace.

energy chart

color: violet • energy center: crown • mantra: i trust •
issues: faith, gratitude, surrender, patience

color: indigo • energy center: brow • mantra: i see •
issues: decisiveness, inspiration, intuition, imagination

color: blue • energy center: throat • mantra: i express •
issues: creativity, communication, sincerity, willpower

color: green • energy center: heart • mantra: i love •
issues: compassion, generosity, peace, forgiveness

color: yellow • energy center: solar plexus • mantra: i know •
issues: empowerment, achievement, self-esteem, information

color: orange • energy center: sacral • mantra: i feel •
issues: pleasure, joy, self-control, well-being

color: red • energy center: root • mantra: i have •
issues: stability, security, safety, balance